Trusting God

THROUGH YOUR RUGGED
TERRAIN

40-Day Devotional

by
SANDREAN HYMAN-HOWARD

Watersprings
PUBLISHING

Trusting God Through Your Rugged Terrain: A 40-day Devotional
published by Watersprings Publishing,
a division of Watersprings Media House, LLC.
P.O. Box 1284 Olive Branch, MS 38654
www.waterspringspublishing.com
Contact the publisher for bulk orders and permission requests.

Copyright © 2024 Sandrean Hyman-Howard. All rights reserved.

No part of this publication may be reproduced, distributed, or transmitted in any form or by any means, including photocopying, recording, or other electronic or mechanical methods, without the prior written permission of the publisher, except in the case of brief quotations embodied in critical reviews and certain other noncommercial uses permitted by copyright law.

Scripture quotations marked (NIV) are taken from the Holy Bible, New International Version, NIV. Copyright ©1973, 1978, 1984, 2011 by Biblica, Inc. Used by permission of Zondervan. All rights reserved worldwide. www.zondervan.com 'The NIV' and 'New International Version' are trademarks registered in the United States Patent and Trademark Office by Biblica, Inc.

Scripture quotations marked (NLT) are taken from the Holy Bible, New Living Translation, copyright © 1996, 2004, 2015 by Tyndale House Foundation. Used by permission of Tyndale House Publishers, Inc., Carol Stream, Illinois 60188. All rights reserved.

Scripture quotations taken from the New American Standard Bible® (NASB), Copyright ©1960,1962,1963,1968,1971,1972,1973,1975,1977,1995 by the Lockman Foundation. Used by permission. www.Lockman.org

Printed in the United States of America.

ISBN-13: 979-8-9894494-5-3

In dedication to my husband, Robert,
my children Leondrae'(Ty) and Serren (Tia) and
my family members and friends.

Thanks to God for inspiration and knowledge.
And to all for the support and encouragement.

TABLE OF CONTENTS

INTRODUCTION 7

Day One: Trust Your Journey 9

Day Two: We May Not See Now 12

Day Three: That New Thing 15

Day Four: From Polka Dots to Spotless 18

Day Five: Feelings 21

Day Six: Unknown Prayers 24

Day Seven: Perfect Timing 27

Day Eight: Misidentified 30

Day Nine: He Will Provide 33

Day Ten: Do Not Be Conformed 36

Day Eleven: The Touch 39

Day Twelve: Shared Prayer 42

Day Thirteen: An Attitude of Gratitude 45

Day Fourteen: Love Extended 48

Day Fifteen: I Am Qualified 51

Day Sixteen: A New Change 54

Day Seventeen: Faith Provision 57

Day Eighteen: Supporting Minds 60

Day Nineteen: Only a Prayer Request 63

Day Twenty: The Power Source 66

Day Twenty One: Personally Known 69

Day Twenty Two: Trust In God 72

Day Twenty Three: Follow the Way 75

Day Twenty Four: The Real One Provided 78

Day Twenty Five: Musical Wind. 81

Day Twenty Six: Tiny Steps 84

Day Twenty Seven: A Prepared Way. 87

Day Twenty Eight: Faithful Promises 90

Day Twenty Nine: Reaping the Harvest 93

Day Thirty: Covered By an Angel 96

Day Thirty One: Never Too Busy 99

Day Thirty Two: Trusting Through the Rugged Terrain. 102

Day Thirty Three: A Very Present Help 105

Day Thirty Four: Decorated Canvas. 108

Day Thirty Five: My Knight in Shining Armor .111

Day Thirty Six: Listen and Obey. 114

Day Thirty Seven: I am Alone But Not Lonely 117

Day Thirty Eight: Just For You. 120

Day Thirty Nine: 'Patience and Trust' – Lessons Learned. 123

Day Forty: God Has the Final Word. .126

ABOUT THE AUTHOR. 129

INTRODUCTION

"I will open rivers in high places, and fountains in the midst of the valleys: I will make the wilderness a pool of water, and the dry land springs of water."

Isaiah 41:18 (KJV)

Being a part of a specific club in my younger years allowed me the privilege of taking hikes and participating in track and trail activities. While participating in these adventures, the journeys were unpredictable. There were times when we traveled on smooth paths that would abruptly change to stony paths. We traveled in valleys, and then we had to climb hills; some were steep, and some were not. Our journeys were directed by trails or signs made by broken twigs or stones. For us to reach the final destination, we needed to know the signs and symbols. They were organized for us to travel in groups, so we were able to help, encourage, and support each other along the way. These experiences gave me the literal feeling as well as a knowledge of different paths taken on a journey. Associating our life's journey to these experiences, I think it is safe to say that we are traveling on a 'rugged terrain.' Life is very unpredictable, as we are unaware of what the next moment will be like.

There are challenges that we encounter daily. We are bombarded with trials, tribulations, storms, disappointments, hurts, discouragements, fears, resentment, and sometimes neglect. On the flip side, we have successes, encouraging moments, happy moments, ups, appointments, and moments of joy. There are times when we are faced with these uncertain moments, we think that we are alone. There is no truth in this thought!

Writing has always been a part of my life as it is one of my hobbies. It is impressed on my heart to share my stories through writing so that others will be encouraged. I decided to be obedient to the voice of the Holy Spirit, so I started putting my pieces together. This was confirmed when I decided to share my writings with others who would seriously encourage me to compile and complete a book. Little did they know that my intentions were in alignment with their thoughts as I had already gotten the inspiration from the Holy Spirit. Another confirmation would come after sharing a devotional; someone would share a song or scripture regarding the exact topic or content that I wrote about.

After reflecting on the many times and ways that God has proven Himself in my life, whether in good or bad times, I am confident that others need motivation or encouragement to help them through these times. God promises us that He will be with us in every situation. He simply wants us to trust Him in all these circumstances. God encourages us in His word through His many promises that He is always with us. He has proven this both in the Bible stories that we read as well as in our lives and the lives of others. In our journey, whether we are going through good times, not-so-good times, or bad times, He is always with us. God is with us through our valley moments, our hilltop seasons, our smooth paths, our rocky steps, and our mountainous journeys. He is always with us and promises never to leave nor forsake us. He is faithful to His words; all we have to do is trust Him. One such promise reminds us:

"Have I not commanded you? Be strong and courageous. Do not be frightened, and do not be dismayed, for the Lord your God is with you wherever you go."

Joshua 1:9 (NIV)

These personal stories that I share serve to encourage you and me as you read and compare my moments with your moments, saying that God will definitely be with you through your rugged terrain. I pray that as you read, you will be inspired, encouraged, and motivated, and you will record your reflections in the space provided so you can use each as a reminder of how God has been with you always and will continue to be with you on your journey. I encourage you to share God with others as we continue to see Him in our everyday lives while we travel on this journey called "Life."

I pray that God will bless you immeasurably and will continue to be with you always. I hope you too will be a blessing to someone else as you share your journey of your rugged terrain.

DAY ONE

TRUST YOUR JOURNEY

"Trust in the LORD with all thine heart, and lean not unto thine own understanding. In all thy ways acknowledge him, and he shall direct thy paths."

Proverbs 3:5-6 (KJV)

I have fallen in love so much with 'journey quotes' and anything positive that says 'faith.' I walked into the store, and as soon as my eye caught the little square frame with the words 'trust your journey' printed boldly on it, I knew I couldn't pass it by. I have been on a journey with God, and I have to trust Him before, during, and after every step of the journey. I had a feeling that this phrase was incomplete, so I searched for the other part that would make it complete. I went on an investigative search for the perfect ending. Ah ha, I thought when I saw a tiny frame, it couldn't have been any more than four by four inches. Even though it was tiny in measurement, the words embossed on the plain canvas made it seem as if it was the biggest thing in the store. 'Faith it, 'till you make it.' Perfect, I thought to myself, now my phrase is complete. I joined the phrase together and repeated it a couple of times. 'Trust your journey, faith it 'till you make it.' Now, this is complete. On this journey, we are blindsided by what our next step will be. We have no clue of what will come on the next step that we take, but we know that for us to move from one place to the next, we have to make that step of faith. One of the promises found in Psalm 91:11 (KJV) reminds us, *"For he shall give His angels charge over thee, to keep thee in all thy ways."* It is comforting to know that we are not on this journey alone. It will automatically become our journey by taking little steps of faith and more little steps of faith and more little steps of faith. We have no clue what the future will bring, so we have to exercise faith and trust our journey. What journey are you about to take that you have to faith it?

The woman with the issue of blood trusted her journey and faithed it until she was healed by touching the hem of the Master's garment.

Moses, with the children of Israel, had to trust their journey and 'faith it till they made it' when they walked through the Red Sea and were safe from Pharaoh's army. Job trusted his journey and faithed it till he made it when he lost everything that he had and was blessed tenfold after. The three Hebrew boys had to trust their journey and faith it till they made it when they were thrown into the fiery furnace and walked out without even the scent of smoke on them. There are numerous stories in the Bible of people who trusted their journey and were able to faith it till they made it. Let us look at it from a personal standpoint. How many of us had to trust our journey and faith it until we made it when we left our house to go somewhere and returned home safely? Do we not trust our journey and faith it till we make it when sickness walks into our homes and the homes of those we love? When the words of termination of jobs caused us the fear of being unable to provide, didn't we trust our journey until we were employed again? When we reflect on our journey, we would not be able to tell tales of the many times we had to trust our journey and faith it till we made it in a day's conversation. Proverbs 3:5-6 (KJV) puts it perfectly by saying, *"Trust in the Lord with all thine heart; and lean not to thine own understanding. In all thy ways acknowledge Him and He shall direct thy paths."* Let us trust our journey and the One who orchestrated the footsteps for the journey and faith it with Him until we make it. Trust God as you use little steps daily, as they will accumulate into something larger. Use these moments as opportunities for growth as we depend on God to take us through to our final destination.

TODAY'S PRAYER

Dear Lord, we thank You for Your words. We thank You for being the only one who has all the future in Your hands and who knows our yesterday, our today, and our tomorrow. Please help us to trust You on our journey, as with faith, we will be able to make it with You. Continue to lead and direct us. We pray and say thanks, in no other name but Jesus, Amen.

REFLECTION

What part of your journey did you, or are you trusting God totally to take control of?

_____

_____

_____

_____

_____

_____

_____

_____

_____

_____

_____

_____

_____

DAY TWO

WE MAY NOT SEE NOW

"Being confident of this, that he who began a good work in you will carry it on to completion until the day of Christ Jesus."

Philippians 1:6 (NIV)

An apartment has become vacant and was on the market for rental. My husband and I were so eager to move from our old apartment as we wanted a bigger apartment. Our addition to the family was due soon, and we needed a bigger space. We contacted the Realtor and completed all our paperwork. We even made an appointment to see the apartment. How excited we were to be finally moving. We prayed and then headed on our way to 'our' new apartment. Upon our arrival, we noticed two other couples who had the same appointment time that we had. 'Oh wow, I guess we're not the only ones who are eager to move, I thought to myself.' Then I consoled myself with, 'Oh Lord, we prayed and asked for this one, and we claim it in Jesus' name.' We continued with the process, asking questions, looking carefully at every detail of the building, and, yes, trying to impress so that we would be the selected ones for the offer. We loved it; we were ready to move in right away. Then came the statement we were not expecting, 'ok, thank you for your time; the owner will review all the applications and will get back to you.' That's not what we wanted to hear. However, we concluded and then departed.

The next day, I called the Realtor, who informed us that no decision had been made yet. I called three days later, but no one answered the phone. We really needed that apartment, so I went in search of the owner. I didn't find him, but I retrieved his phone number from another tenant in the building. I called and left messages continuously until I got him. I spoke very professionally to him, explaining my plight and trying as hard as I could to be the one selected. My disappointment came when he responded that he had collected someone else's deposit the morning, and so it was off the market. I was soooooo disappointed. I was depressed for days; I kept thinking I should have gotten the apartment and questioning what could have prevented us from getting it. I could not sleep because of this ordeal. Psalm 42:11 (ESV) spoke directly to me. It says, *"Why are you cast down, O my soul, and why are you in turmoil within me? Hope in God; for I shall again praise him, my salvation and my God."*

Our baby girl arrived a month early via c-section, so staircases would be out of the question for a while. I reflected on that apartment scenario and accepted the fact that if we had gotten it, I would have to live on the bottom step until after recovery, or I would have to suffer my way, climbing a very narrow flight of fifteen steps and staying in the apartment until after recovery.

God knew the future. God knows the future. There are times we are eager to get something because we are shortsighted, have a tunnel vision and can only see now. We even make our earnest request known unto God and we own it. God who holds our future in His hands knows that this specific thing is not good for us and so he protects us from it. We may not see the protection in the moment but it is always revealed to us after.

Jeremiah 29:11 (NIV) reminds us that, *"For I know the plans I have for you declares the Lord, 'plans to give you hope and a future."* We make our own plans but God's plans far exceeds our own and are best for us. We just need to trust Him.

TODAY'S PRAYER

Dear Lord, please help us to know that You hold our future in Your hands. You have the blueprint of our lives in Your hands and You are the only one who knows the beginning to the end. Help us to trust You when You make plans for our lives and for us to follow You. Amen.

REFLECTION

What plan did God reveal to you that is much better than the plan you had for yourself?

_____

_____

_____

_____

_____

_____

_____

_____

_____

_____

_____

_____

_____

DAY THREE

THAT NEW THING

"Behold, the former things are come to pass, and new things do I declare: before they spring forth I tell you of them."

Isaiah 42:9 (KJV)

The diagnosis has been given, and treatment has begun. A physical is to follow at a given date. The reminder call was made about the date of the physical, and the questions were asked, 'Do I need to do anything special in preparation for this.' Yes, said the nurse, 'this is a fasting physical, so nothing to eat after midnight, and the drink can only be green tea or black coffee, no milk.' I smiled and said, 'Thank you.' Great, I thought to myself, as I don't normally eat after midnight; I have never had coffee, and green tea has become my best friend. So I was merrily on my way, not having to make any major adjustments, or so I thought. Sometimes, there is an ailment inside of us when we do a physical. Whether it be an annual physical or a daily physical. Sometimes, we have to complete a physical because something is happening inside our bodies that we cannot see with the naked eye, and these prevent our bodies from functioning effectively. God has equipped humans with wisdom, knowledge, and understanding that will help us to make these decisions physically. On the other hand, sometimes it is a habit or a continuous negative personality trait that we embrace that prevents us from being effective spiritually or socially. This prevents that positive seed that God has implanted in us for us to flourish and illuminate on the outside. This little seed will thrive and will allow us to be effective, productive, and positive.

Whatever you associate your physical to today: whether it be annual or daily, whether it be spiritual, mental or physical let us choose the positive over the negatives, let us ask God to cleanse us thoroughly from the inside out so that the roots of our little seed can be developed fully allowing the leaves to illuminate on the outside of our bodies and less of us will be seen but more of Him will be portrayed daily.

Isaiah 43:19 (KJV) says, *"Behold, I am doing a new thing, now it shall spring forth, shall ye not know it? I will even make a way in the wilderness and rivers in the desert."*

Let us ask, believe, claim, and receive that new thing that God wants to use in us so we will radiate beauty from the inside today and always.

TODAY'S PRAYER

Dear Jesus, we come asking today for a change inside of us. Forgive us of the sins we have committed so our words will come up to You as sweet incense. Father, we magnify You as our Lord and Savior. Lord, we know that we are fearfully and wonderfully made, and we ask that You help us to live that passage in our daily lives. Help us to trust You as You continue to work out Your will and way for us. We say thanks for hearing and answering our prayer. In Jesus' name, Amen.

REFLECTION

What is the one thing that is preventing that special seed from germinating inside of us?

_____

_____

_____

_____

_____

_____

_____

_____

_____

_____

_____

_____

DAY FOUR
FROM POLKA DOTS TO SPOTLESS

"Therefore if anyone is in Christ, this person is a new creation; the old things passed away; behold, new things have come."

2 Corinthians 5:17 (NASB)

Washing is a state of art that requires some work and some patience. My girlfriend accompanied my daughter and I to an activity dressed in sparkling white slacks. After a few hours of returning home, I noticed some blue polka dots on her pants and asked what happened to her clean pants. At first, she did not know what really happened, but after retracing her activities, she remembered that she was using a gel ink pen that leaked all over her pants in multiple locations. I told her the remedy for that which my husband had done with my son's messy clothes situations with ink before, which requires just a soak in rubbing alcohol.

The next day, my girlfriend started telling me that her pants seemed to be no good anymore. She continued to express how much she loved her pants and she wished she could do something to get the stains out. She went further to express that the rubbing alcohol only made it worse and how much she loved those pants and wanted to get the stains out. A love for pants is what she really has. Because she kept repeating that statement, it is very obvious she loved it. She showed me the effect that she had gotten, and it was indeed not looking good. It really looked as if it was ready now to go in the trash. I told her to put some more rubbing alcohol and then spray some bleach on it.

She quickly did that (because she loved her pants and really wanted to save it). My friend who was never musically inclined became a singer as a heard a melodious tune from the bathroom, 'I got back my pants, oh I got back my pants.' She then proceeded out to show me the pants now which looked like a brand-new pants, to be honest it looked even better than before it got the stains on it.

When we are burdened down, torn, weary, sickened, dreary, frustrated, and angry, sin takes over our lives. We have a God who loves us unconditionally and is able to pick us up, turn us around, turn us inside out, forgive our sins, and plant our feet on higher ground. Isaiah 1:18 (KJV) states, *"Come now, and let us reason together, saith the Lord: though your sins be as scarlet, they shall be as white as snow; though they be red like crimson, they shall be as wool."* The color scarlet explains to us the stain that is left upon our souls after we have sinned. That stain is a representation of the blue ink stain on my girlfriend's pants. However, that stain can be removed with God's forgiveness. Whenever His work is complete in us, we are brand new, even better than before. Whatever our situation is today, God is asking us to trust His work in us as He creates a clean heart and renews a right Spirit within us.

TODAY'S PRAYER

Dear Lord, we ask You today to bless us far more than we are able to ask, think, or imagine as You continue to work on us and make us better than we were the day before. Continue to wash and make us whiter than snow. We ask in the name of Jesus, and say thanks in advance, Amen.

REFLECTION

God is able to do far more than we can imagine. What is it that you want Him to amaze you with?

_____

_____

_____

_____

_____

_____

_____

_____

_____

_____

_____

_____

_____

_____

DAY FIVE

FEELINGS

"The LORD is close to the brokenhearted; he rescues those whose spirits are crushed."

Psalm 34:18 (NLT)

Rejection, resentment, betrayal, denial, abuse: are these a part of the famous 'Love Story'? Oftentimes, these are some of the meals that are served to us on a silver platter around the table with a knife, fork, and a well-folded napkin. Did we deserve it? Is it a part of God's plan? How can we move forward? Should we feel bad about it? Rejection, resentment, betrayal, denial, and abuse are negative behaviors that hurt to the core. It does not go away very easily. These are hurtful feelings that are handed to us most of the time by family members, friends, coworkers, and, sad to say, church members. One writer says, 'Don't worry about your enemy, but be **very** concerned about the ones who say, 'I love you.'' That's when it hurts the most, when you expect your ride or die, your spouse, your best friend, to be there for you. But, instead of being loved and cared for, you get that reaction of rejection, resentment, betrayal, denial, and abuse. Oh, how it hurts.

Sometimes, it is hand-delivered to us when life knocks us to the curb with sickness, when we lose a job, when we lose a family member, or when we are going through our midlife crisis. When we need that extra prayer to make us stronger, when we need that extra ear to listen to us, when we need that extra heart to love us, when we need that extra eye to see for us, when we need that extra hand to hold us and when we need that extra foot to help us walk. That is when we feel rejection, resentment, betrayal, denial, and abuse the most.

The Bible speaks how Jesus was rejected by the ones with Him, Samson was rejected by Delilah, Joseph was rejected by his brothers, Stephen was rejected by the church, Noah was rejected by the people whom he preached to for one hundred and twenty years, and Leah was rejected by her father, Laban. These people were also blessed immeasurably after that period of rejection. As the scripture rightly puts it in Psalm 118:22 (NASB), *"A stone that the builders rejected has become the chief cornerstone."*

Are you feeling rejected, resented, betrayed, denied, and abused? It hurts, I know, and it hurts deeply, but we can be comforted in the word where it says in Psalm 27:10 (NLT), *"Even if my mother and my father abandon me, the Lord will pick me up,"* and *Psalm 94:14 (NLT), "for the Lord will not reject his people, he will not abandon his special possession."* God will be with us all the way. He is the only one who loves us unconditionally.

TODAY'S PRAYER

Dear Lord, thank You for Your unconditional love towards us. Thank You for never letting us feel rejected, resented, betrayed, denied, or abused. Help us when these feelings come that they won't take away our peace, and we won't let them define us, but we will cast our cares upon You because You truly care for us. Amen.

REFLECTION

What resentment or rejection are you experiencing now that you can give to Jesus?

_____

_____

_____

_____

_____

_____

_____

_____

_____

_____

_____

_____

_____

DAY SIX

UNKNOWN PRAYERS

"I urge, then, first of all, that petitions, prayers, intercession and thanksgiving be made for all people."

1 Timothy 2:1 (NIV)

On a hot summer's day, my husband and I decided to take a walk in the late afternoon when it was a little cooler. We strolled maybe for three blocks or so, talking about the day's activities and some plans we had to execute for the days ahead. While heading across the street to our house, we heard a voice ask, 'Are you okay?' I quickly turned around, and instead of answering yes or no, I replied with the question, 'Why do you ask that?' The lady responded by saying, ' I saw that you lost weight.' This is my neighbor; I remember seeing the younger people that live at the house, but I don't remember ever seeing this lady. I proceeded by introducing myself and my husband to her, and she did the same. After that, I answered her question, 'No, I am not okay; I have been sick.' I explained briefly what my illness was, which developed into a lengthy conversation as she could relate to an extent as she expressed that her sister had the same illness. She also explained that she works in the medical field and is familiar with the condition that I have.

She went on to make a very profound statement, one that I was really not expecting. She said, 'I saw that you were not well, and I have been praying for you. '(Remember I have never seen this lady).

This lady exemplified that she is a true ambassador of Christ. James 5:16 (KJV) says, *"confess your faults one to another, and pray one for another, that ye may be healed. The effectual fervent prayer of a righteous man availeth much."* James knows how powerful prayer is, and he wanted us to know this, too. Praying for others is an act that we care for others. I thanked her greatly, spoke for a short while, concluded the conversation, and then went home. As I thought about the conversation we had, I don't know her, and she doesn't know me. She saw me and knew I did not look the way I did before, so she has been praying for me. That was the greatest gift anyone could offer me during this period.

God has placed people we know, people who know us and we don't know them, or people we know and who don't know us in our lives at the right time, for the right reason or season. We have our Red Sea experience that we will go through, but God has already prepared the way for us to walk as well as genuine people who will stand by us, encouraging and motivating us, but most important of all, those who will be praying for and with us.

Prayer is an action that is never too much, never too little, never too short, and never too limited to only everyone. It can be extended to even those we have never even heard of. It is the key that unlocks heaven's storehouse. Let us continue to use this method to build our relationship with our maker as well as to petition for others - both known and unknown.

1 Timothy 2:1 (NLT) also tells us, *"First of all, to pray for all people. Ask God to help them; intercede on their behalf, and give thanks for them."* Praying for others builds our spiritual muscles. Prayer makes a difference and helps us take our burdens to our Great, Big, Wonderful God. God's words say we can have confidence that when we pray, He hears us, and we have the petitions we desire of Him. Let us choose to give someone the gift of prayer today, as this can be a powerful blessing for them.

TODAY'S PRAYER

Dear Lord, thank You so much for hearing the prayers of those who prayed for me and others. Someone prayed for me; I'm so glad they prayed for me, and I am excited that You heard their prayers. Help us to always share the gift of praying for others. Amen.

REFLECTION

Who is one person that you have been praying for, and how do you see God working?

_____

_____

_____

_____

_____

_____

_____

_____

_____

_____

_____

_____

_____

_____

DAY SEVEN

PERFECT TIMING

"He has made everything beautiful in its time. He has also set eternity in the human heart, yet no one can fathom what God has done from beginning to end."

Ecclesiastes 3:11 (NIV)

I had a taste for a specific meal that I had requested from my girlfriend. She prepared it and sent it to me via my husband. It was so delicious I had to try it again. I knew I had to prepare the meal this time as she was at work and would be busy for the entire week. I plugged my phone into the charger to get more battery life, and I realized it was about thirty percent charged. I had to go to the store to get the items I wanted so I could prepare my lunch. I peeked outside to test the weather and was greeted with dancing trees and running leaves on the ground. Despite not feeling well, I layered up so I would be prepared for the party that was sponsored by the wind and the cold outside. I requested a taxi service, and it took three minutes to arrive. I unplugged my phone and realized that it wasn't charging; the same thirty percent that I had before I plugged it in was the same -nothing more, nothing less. 'What am I going to do now?' I thought. I can't leave the phone because I need it to request a return taxi. I will need it for confirmation from my friend that I am making the correct purchase, and I need it in case of an emergency. Then, the thought came into my head that I should turn it off until I needed it. I quickly obeyed, as I didn't want to be stuck outdoors.

I arrived at the store and started searching but could not find what I wanted. My next choice was to call my girlfriend, which I did, and that was successful. I, however, didn't remember to turn my phone off again. I shopped for another ten minutes, and then it was time for me to go home. I went outside and requested the car. The car was requested, information regarding the description of the car was received, and the phone was blank. I tried to turn it on again, but nothing happened as the battery had died.

What an awesome God I serve. He knew I needed to get information and get home, so he kept the phone on so I would get just that. He allowed the battery to be off at the perfect time. I was able to trust God in His timing. I knew that God would come through for me in this moment. We go through situations in life, and things fall through or come through at the perfect timing. God is an on-time God, and if we only be patient, we will definitely reap the rewards. Let us cast our burdens at His feet because He cares for us and will give us that peace that we need. God's timing is impeccably perfect and also impossible to predict. David reminds us in Psalm 27: 14 (KJV), *"Wait on the Lord: be of good courage, and he shall strengthen thine heart: wait, I say, on the Lord."* He will come through for us. One songwriter says, 'He's an on-time God, yes He is. He may not come when you want Him, but He'll be there right on time. He's an on-time God, yes He is.' This day was another proof that He's an on-time God. I want to be patient with Him as He works out the steps in my life. Won't you be patient with Him too?

TODAY'S PRAYER

Dear Lord, we thank You for being our Father, and I ask that You create a clean heart in us and forgive us of our sins. We are confident that You have orchestrated every step of our lives carefully to fit us individually. Please give us the patience and peace that we need as You execute Your plans in Your own timing. Help us to trust You more, I pray. Thank You for loving us unconditionally. We pray in Jesus' name, Amen.

REFLECTION

What is one way that God is showing you that He orchestrated your steps?

_____
_____
_____
_____
_____
_____
_____
_____
_____
_____
_____
_____

DAY EIGHT

MISIDENTIFIED

"But now thus saith the Lord that created thee, O Jacob, and he that formed thee, O Israel, Fear not: for I have redeemed thee, I have called thee by thy name; thou art mine."

Isaiah 43:1 (KJV)

'The ants go marching one by one, oorah, oorah,' echoed the song my toddler keeps listening to. As I lay in bed, unable to do much due to health problems, I had to revise the song's words. This is how I have to sing it, 'The bills keep coming one by one, oorah, oorah.' This wasn't the happiest song for me to sing as the costs attached to them were very expensive. It was one of my husband's happiest chores to complete when he got home if I wasn't energized enough to do it during the daytime - collect the mail. He literally took two or more bills to me every day, so I joked with my sister about calling me 'Billy.'

There is one specific billing company that I received not one, not two, not three, not four, but five different bills. One bill was for over three thousand dollars, one was for three hundred dollars, two were for over two hundred dollars, and the other was for over one hundred dollars. They were all attached to different extension numbers. One month before getting these bills, I called the number in the mail and was directed to the billing department. Unfortunately, the Representative was having technical difficulties with her phone line. She promised to get the issue corrected and return my call so I could make the payment. She did follow through, but I missed the call. I called the next day and a few more days after, but the phone only went to her voicemail. I decided to give it a break for a day. The next day, when I called, I was greeted with the prerecorded message that they were closed for two days for a religious holiday. I patiently waited for that time to pass, and then I called again but was unsuccessful in getting at least one of my bills paid again. I kept looking at the numbers on the bills, and my concern was about getting them out of the way, especially the larger bills.

My aunt visited me from another country, and I explained to her my medical financial responsibilities. At that point, I took up the phone and dialed the number again, and sure enough, it was the prerecorded message again informing me that they were closed for another religious holiday. 'Oh well, I thought, these people don't want their money, and I have a use for it.'

When my aunt was done inspecting the bills, she asked, 'Why does this bill have a different name and address on it? To my surprise, I was sent another person's bill. Unfortunately, it was not the biggest one. I paused for a moment and thanked God for all the disappointments I had trying to pay these bills and for allowing my aunt the insight to see the mistake. Even though the Billing Company sent me someone else's bill, God knows me by name, and He knows everything about me. In Isaiah 43:1 (NIV), God says to Moses, *"Fear not, for I have redeemed you; I have summoned you by name; you are mine."* God is giving us that same promise today. He is showing us that He claims us as His own. It shows us that God has a personal relationship with us.

Jeremiah 1:5 (NASB), *"Before I formed you in the womb I knew you, and before you were born I consecrated you; I have appointed you a prophet to the nations."* We don't have to be concerned about an identity crisis with Jesus. He created us and paid for our sins. When He died on the cross, He had you, me, and everyone else on His mind. Sometimes things happen, and we are so disappointed, but then, after divine insight, careful assessment, or advice from someone else, we realize that we were saved from something bad and have been given a divine appointment. God gives us these lessons to understand that we don't have to worry about our blessings being given to someone else or someone else's blessings given to us as He knows everything about us as even the very hair on our head is numbered and we are more valuable to God than a whole flock of sparrows. Let us trust Him, who is our Creator and the guide to our daily lives.

TODAY'S PRAYER

Dear Lord, thank You for being our Creator and for guiding us daily. Search us, O Lord, and remove all unworthiness from us. Lord, help us to keep our trust in You as You know everything about us and will never mistake us for another. Help us to take disappointments for appointments as You lead and direct our lives. Continue to be our guide and help us to keep our eyes fixed on You as we follow Your lead. We praise Your matchless name and say thanks for leading us. In Jesus' name, we pray, Amen.

REFLECTION

Briefly explain one scenario when you were disappointed and you realized that it worked out for your good.

_____
_____
_____
_____
_____
_____
_____
_____
_____
_____
_____

DAY NINE

HE WILL PROVIDE

"Now to Him who is able to do far more abundantly beyond all that we ask or think, according to the power that works within us."

Ephesians 3:20 (NASB)

Struggling from day to day to be physically healthy for over a year wasn't enough torture for her. She was placed on short-term disability from her place of employment, which has now expired. She was placed on long-term disability. She had to complete progress forms for her job ever so often and submit them back via mail, email, or personal drop-off at her place of employment. Early one Friday morning, her boss texted her with some important information regarding the long-term disability process and to query how she was feeling physically.

She replied honestly that some days, she felt like she was getting better, and some days, she felt like she was not. She also informed her that she was taking the form to the office. Her boss then questioned what time she would be there and if she was coming solo and then closed the phone conversation. She got to the office and went up to the fourth floor with her husband, where the office is located. She was greeted with a warm embrace as soon as the door of the elevator was opened. She was then directed to the closest conference room so as not to attract any unnecessary attention from the other employees. Her boss, who is also the Human Resource Director, started her well-planned speech by asking again how she was feeling and how was her recovery. Again, she responded that some days, she felt like she was getting better, some days, she felt like she was not.

Her boss continued the conversation by saying that the employee had been sick for approximately six months, and they were not able to hold the position for her any longer, and they would have to terminate her. She explained further that they had been hiring temporary workers for the six-month period, and the company was being affected by the numerous changes they had to make during this time. A million things started flashing across her mind as she tried to process the statement she just heard. 'How will she help finance her family's needs? She was really anticipating going back to work. Was it considerate to add one more stressor on her, even in her time of sickness? Where is the empathy?' After sitting in shock and silence for a few minutes, her boss asked if she had anything to say. Through her cracked voice and the tears trickling down her cheeks, she managed to say, 'Thank you,' and then she dismissed herself. Even though she was trying very hard not to, she went home feeling very discouraged, broken, and betrayed. A good friend called to see how she was doing and encouraged her with the words that God did not create us to be independent.

We were created to be dependent on God. He gave us promises to use as encouragement in times of brokenness. When we choose to put God at the center of our lives, he will always provide what we need spiritually, mentally, physically, financially, academically and psychologically. He understands our needs better than we do and He truly cares for us.

God allows doors to be closed so he can open a bigger and better one. He promised us in His words that *"He shall supply all our needs according to his riches in glory by Christ Jesus."* Philippians 4:19 (NKJV). David also tells us in Psalm 37:25 (KJV), *"I have been young, and now am old; yet have I not seen the righteous forsaken, nor his seed begging bread."* When God allows these trials, He already has His plans to help us see our way through. We must cast our cares at His feet and trust Him to do the rest for us. Even when we can't see our way through, He will provide. He cannot and will not lie about the promises He gave us.

TODAY'S PRAYER

Dear Lord, we are privileged to call you Father, Friend, and Redeemer. Please help us to seek You first in our lives and You will add everything according to Your will and riches to us. Please help us to trust You daily, as You will never go back on Your word and You will come through for us. Thank You for reaching out to us in a state where no one else is able to reach us. We magnify Your Holy name and say thanks, in Jesus' name, Amen.

REFLECTION

What does God promise to do when we seek Him first?

_____

_____

_____

_____

_____

_____

_____

_____

_____

_____

_____

_____

_____

DAY TEN
DO NOT BE CONFORMED

"And be not conformed to this world: but be ye transformed by the renewing of your mind, that ye may prove what is that good, and acceptable, and perfect, will of God."

Romans 12:2 (KJV)

For family worship this specific morning, we decided to speak freely about a religious topic. Whatever topic we chose, we would also take the opportunity to encourage the other family members. The topic I suddenly selected with the help of the Holy Spirit was about our thoughts. Explaining carefully that what we see, hear, watch, and the places we go impact what we think. Most times, our thoughts become our actions. The next day, our family decided to go to our regular church, and then we would visit another church that had a special speaker whom we enjoyed listening to whenever he preached. At our regular church, the speaker spoke carefully about the scripture Romans 12:2 (NIV), *"Do not be conformed to this world, but be transformed by the renewing of our mind. Then you will be able to test and approve what God's will is- His good, pleasing and perfect will."* We then went to the second church. Guess what the speaker spoke about? Yes, yes, you guessed it correctly. Romans 12:2. He went a little further to explain that we should be careful of our thoughts because our thoughts eventually become our actions. A lesson it was indeed.

Driving home, we got stuck in the passing lane on the highway behind a very slow truck. We switched lanes, but on the dark tinted windows, written in white were the familiar words, 'Do not be conformed to this world' in Lucinda script writing. God, this must be a lesson you're trying to teach us from this scripture. Would you believe me if I tell you that when I reached home and tuned in online to a different church in a different country, I was just in time to hear the speaker reading the scripture verse Romans 12:2. A confirmation it is indeed that God wants me, wants my family, wants us all to be not conformed by the world but be transformed (be changed) by the renewing of our minds. We will be able to test and prove what God's will is for us.

We live in this world with a lot of nice things, places that seem fun, words that sound good, fashion that looks good, and actions that feel good. But they go contrary to God's will for our lives. As children of the King, we are encouraged to feast on God's words and hide them in our hearts, as well as build a closer relationship with our heavenly Father so that He can transform us to do His will in our lives. What 'little thing' that we embrace that is holding us from being transformed. Is it our jobs, social media, friends, and television shows that keep us from spending time with God so we can be changed? Whatever it is, God is excitedly waiting for us to give them to Him so He can exchange them for Godly transformation so He can work His will in us. Why don't you give Him a chance and prove Him to transform your life today?

TODAY'S PRAYER

Dear God, we thank You for Your promise in Romans 12:2, that You will change us to do Your will in our lives. God, we are tired of being the same every day and not being able to change ourselves, no matter how hard we try. God, please give us the strength to be able to give You 'the world' in us so you can change it for Your will. Do a new thing in our lives as we keep our thoughts heavenward. Thank You for Your divine will and purpose for our lives. Help us to live it out daily and to give You honor and praise. In Jesus' name, Amen.

REFLECTION

What worldly habit are you distracted by that is preventing you from being transformed?

_____

_____

_____

_____

_____

_____

_____

_____

_____

_____

_____

DAY ELEVEN

THE TOUCH

"Everyone tried to touch him, because healing power went out from him, and he healed everyone."

Luke 6:19 (NLT)

Laying in the hospital bed after a long day with meetings with different teams that are trying to figure out the status of my health condition, the effectiveness or ineffectiveness of the current treatment, and the best prospective treatment that will prevent having to do a major surgery and other in-house meetings, my body was exhausted. I have been praying for healing, and my church family, locally and internationally, have been placing their petitions before God for healing. I believe with all my heart that I am already healed, but I just have to go through the process.

I decided to take a nap after all the activities were completed. I plugged my headphones in my ears and started listening to some of my favorite gospel songs. Before you know it I was totally knocked out.

In my sleep, I had an experience that was second to none. I was lying on my left side, and I had my left arm up on my body. I felt like my arm was falling off, so I pulled it back on. Then I felt gentle electric shocks from my left toe traveling all the way up to my arms, then my shoulder, around my head, to my shoulder, then in my right arm, and down to my right leg. Then I saw a female image come in and touched my tummy, and then a male figure appeared and kissed me on my tummy. The kiss was a very long one, and I decided to ease the lips off the troubled area of my body, which is my stomach area. I literally moved my hand to the image, but when I did, my hand went right through the image and straight onto the blanket. Then, the nurse called and woke me up for my medication.

God reveals Himself to us in prophecy, in visions, and in dreams, as is repeatedly spoken of in scriptures. Joel 2:28-29 (NIV) tells us, *"And afterward, I will pour out my Spirit on all people Your sons and daughters will prophesy, your old men will dream dreams, your young men will see visions. Even on my servants, both men and women, I will pour out my Spirit in those days."*

God communicates with us through different ways. Joseph was a dreamer, Moses was a dreamer, and Joseph among many others were spoken to by God through dreams. I am still in awe but I know the Holy Spirit has worked, is working and will continue to work. God knew that I needed that touch from him to heal me of my wounds.

He promised us in His words in Psalm 147:3 (KJV), *"He healeth the broken in heart and bindeth up their wounds."* In Isaiah 53:5 (KJV), *"He was wounded for our transgressions he was bruised for our iniquities, the chastisement of our peace was upon Him and by his stripes we are healed."* He also promised in Luke 6:19 (NASB), *"And all the people were trying to touch him: for power was coming from Him and healing them all."*

Jesus has not changed. He's the same, yesterday and forever. It applies to us now, too. We just need to ask, believe, claim, and receive it in Jesus' name. Just one touch and we are healed. He is still the Great Physician who still works on our behalf; we just have to trust Him.

TODAY'S PRAYER

Dear Lord, we are so thankful that You are the great Physician. Please forgive us for all our sins. Thank You for reminding us that there is a Balm in Gilead to make the wounded whole and to heal the sin-sick soul. Just like the woman at the well who was healed, You will heal us also. We ask for not only a physical healing but also for spiritual healing as You transform our lives. Thank You for your healing wonders in Jesus name, Amen.

REFLECTION

Explain a time that you needed a touch from Jesus. Did you receive healing?

_____

_____

_____

_____

_____

_____

_____

_____

_____

_____

_____

DAY TWELVE
SHARED PRAYER

"Who comforts us in all our afflictions, so that we are able to comfort them who are in any affliction with the comfort with which we ourselves are comforted by God."

2 Corinthians 1:4 (NASB)

With excitement, the nurse rushed in to say that they had a room available, so I will be moving to the sixth floor shortly. I was excited because I could get a little more privacy than the holding area I was in. I arrived at my new room to see an elderly lady as my roommate was having lunch. After I settled into what I call my 'hospitel' (a cross between hospital and hotel) room, I introduced myself to her. We spoke briefly about our conditions, and then I retired to bed. Things changed; however, the next day my roommate was discharged, and a different roommate was assigned to me. She would not allow me to get any rest, whether day or night, due to her constant outbursts, so I prayed for her and requested a change. A change it surely was as this room was very tiny and allowed no room for privacy.

My roommate was an elderly lady and very quiet, and again, I introduced myself to her. She moaned every time the pain attacked her body. I listened to her sadly and was prompted by the Holy Spirit to pray with her. I started dozing, and I got another prompting, so I got up quickly and asked if I could pray with her. She gladly accepted, and so I petitioned the throne on her behalf. She was so happy I did and expressed how thankful she was. The next day, she was discharged. Wow, all my roommates are leaving me here, I thought. But God had a plan for me, and I was not leaving the hospital until that plan was fully executed.

2 Corinthian 1:4 (NASB) states, *"Who comforts us in all our afflictions, so that we are able to comfort them who are in any affliction with the comfort with which we ourselves are comforted by God."*

When we pray for and bless others, a blessing also returns to us. I was praying for my roommate, and in return, I was praying for my own healing through the comfort that I received from God.

The most important gift we can offer anyone is the gift of prayer, as prayer does change things. In praying for healing for my roommate, I was being healed through selfless prayer. Let us continue to pray for others so our hearts will be blessed in return. Jesus longs for us to minister to others and to tell them of His unconditional love for them. He wants to save us; He comes that we may have life and that we may have it more abundantly.

TODAY'S PRAYER

Dear Lord, thank You for the opportunity that we still have to pray for others. So many people still yearn for You, dear Lord. Give us the courage to approach others when we are impressed to pray for them. Cleanse us from all unrighteousness so Your light will shine through us. We thank You in Jesus' name, Amen.

REFLECTION

Have you been impressed to pray for someone you see but don't know them? Did you obey, and how did you feel after the prayer?

_____

_____

_____

_____

_____

_____

_____

_____

_____

_____

_____

_____

_____

_____

DAY THIRTEEN
AN ATTITUDE OF GRATITUDE

"Rejoice always, pray continually, and give thanks in all circumstances; for this is God's will for you in Christ Jesus."

1 Thessalonians 5:16-18 (NIV)

One songwriter penned the words of the song we often convincingly sing, 'There's a roof up above me, 'A good place to sleep, There's food on my table, and shoes on my feet, You gave me Your love, Lord, and a fine family; Thank You, Lord, for Your blessings on me.'

When you sit at the table, what are you thankful for? What was your response to this question? Did you reply by saying?

I am thankful for food.

I am thankful for good grades.

I am thankful for family and friends.

I am thankful that I have a job.

I am thankful for my house.

All these are great responses but let us take a moment to look at some other important reasons why we, why I am thankful. I am thankful for life. In John 10:10 (NIV) it says, *"The thief comes to kill and destroy but I have come that they may have life, and have it to the full."*

After my one-week anniversary of leaving the hospital after being hospitalized for two weeks, this began a new life for me because along with healing, prayer, and medication that God gave the Doctors wisdom to treat me with, I am now home again with my family to build more memories as we celebrate another Thanksgiving with family and friends. I am now able to be at home and worship with my church family again.

I am thankful Jesus died on the cross to save us from our sins. John 3:16

(KJV) says, *"For God so loved the world that He gave His only begotten Son, that whosoever believeth in Him should not perish but have everlasting life."* We are so important to Jesus so much that when He was on the cross, we were on His mind. He called us His masterpiece. I am thankful to have praying family and friends. People are placed in our lives for a reason. When God selected our family and friends, He didn't just choose anyone for us, but He selected the best fit that we would need at every stage of our lives. He selected the very ones who would pray earnestly for us, the ones who would love us no matter what, and the ones who would support us continuously. 1 Peter 2:9 (KJV) states, *"But you are a chosen generation, a royal priesthood, a holy nation, His own special people that you may proclaim the praises of Him that called you out of darkness into this marvelous light."*

Each person was placed in their own royal realm. As I recount my blessings, I could go on and on, and I am sure you can, too. Let us not only wait for Thanksgiving Day to be grateful but let us cultivate an attitude of gratitude daily. As we practice this, we improve our relationship with God, develop our self-worth and self-esteem, build better relationships, and enhance our physical being.

Developing gratitude makes us feel more joyful and fulfilled every day. Let us count our blessings and name them one by one daily, whether big or small.

TODAY'S PRAYER

Dear Lord, we just want to thank You for everything. We give You thanks for the small things, big things, simple things, and complex things, just everything. Help us to develop a daily attitude of gratitude as this will help us to bring us closer to You. Amen.

REFLECTION

Write a list of things you are thankful for. Express gratitude for these things.

_____

_____

_____

_____

_____

_____

_____

_____

_____

_____

_____

_____

DAY FOURTEEN

LOVE EXTENDED

"For God so loved the world that He gave His only begotten Son, that whosoever believeth in Him should not perish but have everlasting life."

John 3:16 (KJV)

I love you, I love you, I LOVE YOU. These are three famous words that have been expressed by family members, friends, coworkers, acquaintances, and even sometimes toward people that we just met. It is a very common expression. Do we truly know the full meaning of love?

Do we display the love we commonly say that we have? I often tell others that I rather show or be shown love more than just to say or hear, 'I love you.' Love, as described in Merriam-Webster's Dictionary, is a verb (an action word) and means to 'show affection, to value highly and to feel the passion.' Love is not expressed on conditions, nor can I only show you love if you show me love. God gave us the greatest example of showing us how to love in John 3:16 (KJV). It says, *"For God so loved the world that He gave His only begotten Son, that whosoever believeth in Him should not perish but have everlasting life."* Because of our sinful nature, we could not, will not, and cannot do anything to merit His love for us. He expresses His love for us because He is our Creator and because He loves us unconditionally. He expresses His love for us daily by providing for us, protecting us, waking us up, keeping us in our right minds, and bringing us brand new mercies for each new day.

Have we, at any point, been shown love? It is indeed a wonderful feeling, isn't it?

> God has placed me in an environment with an awesome support group. Love showed up at my house to pray for my family and me.
>
> Love fasted and prayed for my healing.

Love brought cooked and uncooked food to my house.

Love supported my family and me with financial gifts when I lost my job in the middle of my illness.

Love took the kids home and to church when I was in the hospital.

Love called me and sent me text messages of encouragement.

Love visited me when I was in the hospital.

Love traveled internationally to take care of me when I was sick.

Love was extended to me, and because I have God's love in me, I intend to extend all the love I have in me to someone else.

1 Corinthians 13:4-7 (NIV) says, *"Love is patient, love is kind, it does not envy, it does not boast, it is not proud, it is not rude, it is not self-seeking, it is not easily angered, it keeps no record of wrongs. Love does not delight in evil but rejoices with the truth. It always protects, always trusts, always hopes, and always perseveres."* Love basically never fails.

By following this list, we can confidently say we have extended love to someone. It is a great feeling to love and be loved. Let us hold on to the scripture in 1 John 4:7 (NASB), which says, *"Beloved let us love one another, for love is from God; and everyone who loves is born of God and knows God."*

TODAY'S PRAYER

Dear Lord, we come before Your Holy throne, lifting Your name on high. We accept You as our Lord and Savior and thank You for the example of unconditional love You gave us by sending Your Son, Jesus, to die on the cross for our sins. Lord, You created us, bought us, and redeemed us. No love is greater than Your love, O Lord. Please show us how to love as we live daily. We adore Your matchless name and say thank You in no other name but Jesus' name, Amen.

REFLECTION

How do you feel when you express love to someone or when you receive love from someone?

_____

_____

_____

_____

_____

_____

_____

_____

_____

_____

_____

_____

DAY FIFTEEN

I AM QUALIFIED

"For we are God's handiwork, created in Christ Jesus to do good works, which God prepared in advance for us to do."

Ephesians 2:10 (NIV)

I opened my email with anticipation of receiving positive feedback from at least one of the organizations to whom I had sent my resume and cover letter for a job they advertised. Before that, I spent hours updating my resume to ensure the information presented would be appealing enough to land me that specific job. I requested the opinions of others who would proofread and assist me with edits. Finally, I envisioned myself sitting at that particular company's desk wearing a badge that describes my job title and performing my duties well. My heart sank in despair as I read the words, *'Thanks so much for your application and interest in the (blank) role here at (blank). After review, we will not be moving forward with your candidacy - we have received many qualified applicants and will be considering candidates we feel better fit this role and what we're looking for. Thanks again for your interest, and we hope for all the best in your job search!'*

No part of me was spared as one after the other, the rejection emails came with similar rhetoric. To be honest, in some of the jobs I had applied to, the rejection did not matter. I just applied to get out of the house and do something. The discouragement mainly came from the ones that I was really excited about because of the company's name or the fancy job title that I would be wearing so proudly, that sounded like music when the words rolled off my tongue and that I felt like I was qualified enough to be great at my job.

I questioned the company's decision, *'After review, we will not be moving forward with your candidacy - we have received many qualified applicants and will be moving forward in considering candidates whom we feel better fit this role and what we're looking for,'* as it kept playing in my head like a scratched record.

The feeling of inadequacy and rejection held me down for a while. Rejection is not a pleasant feeling that can sometimes scar us for a time. But the things that we're sometimes rejected for by others do not disqualify us before God. I was encouraged by 2 Corinthians 3:5 (NLT), which says, "*It is not that we think we are qualified to do anything on our own. Our qualifications come from God.*"

I reflected on some of the persons in the Bible who felt rejection. First of all, Jesus Himself felt rejected from His family, community, and even us. Moses' stutter made him feel so unqualified that he asked God to pick someone else to lead the Israelites Exodus (4:10-13). Jesus' disciples were such unlikely choices that the council described them as unschooled, ordinary men Acts (4:13). David was told he was a child and that Goliath would crush him. Yet he was the one that God used to defeat the giant 1 Samuel (17:1-58), and Jephthah was sent away because he was considered an outcast, but God used him to be the liberator of His people Judges (11:1-33).

We often live with the sense that unless we possess specific skills or qualifications, we will not be able to measure up. We think that without the proper credentials or having the letters of the alphabet behind our names, we are considered not enough. We often create our own plans in our heads, but Proverbs 19:21 (NIV) reminds us that *"many are the plans in a person's heart, but the Lord's purpose prevails."*

We feel rejected when we're denied the privilege of doing what we want. What allows you to feel rejected or to feel like you are unqualified? Do you struggle with wondering if you're enough? My friend, it is comforting to know that Jesus knows exactly what you're feeling as He, too, felt the pain of rejection. Take courage that Jesus redeemed us by taking the rejection all over again and covering it in grace that you're qualified to receive any and every blessing from God not because of our limitations but because of God's greatness. You're qualified because Jesus paid the price to qualify us all. It is a gift to all. We have to accept Him and receive it. Trust in Him as He will complete the good work that He has started in your life to live out His divine purpose.

TODAY'S PRAYER

Dear Jesus, please forgive us for our sins. Thank You for Your promises to remind us that we're more than enough and that You qualify us by redeeming us. Remind us when we feel inadequate that we can do everything through You, who strengthens us. Help us to be confident in Your words over our lives and know our identity in You. Help us to be reminded that we are children of the Most High. We open our hearts and accept You as our example. We bless Your name and say thanks for hearing and answering our plea in Jesus' name, Amen.

REFLECTION

At what time in your life have you felt unqualified? What promise can you speak over your life to encourage yourself?

_____
_____
_____
_____
_____
_____
_____
_____
_____
_____
_____
_____

DAY SIXTEEN

A NEW CHANGE

"Therefore we do not lose heart. Though outwardly we are wasting away, yet inwardly we are being renewed day by day."

2 Corinthians 4:16 (KJV)

Poinsettias are famously known to be around at Christmas time. I am a lover, maybe because they are red and red is my favorite color. Approximately three weeks before Christmas, I bought myself a poinsettia plant at the store. After searching vigorously, I was unsuccessful because they only had a few artificial potted plants. Two Saturdays before Christmas, I had a thank-you gift for my girlfriend in the car. My family and I had driven to the city for homecoming Sabbath at my son's school, so I communicated with my girlfriend for a mutual meet-up location so I could deliver my gift to her.

We exchanged gifts, and I was excited to see that she gave me a natural poinsettia plant. I had no conversation with her previously about my desire for a poinsettia plant, nor was I expecting a gift from her. She really made my day. I took the best care of that plant by watering it, putting it in the sunlight, cleaning the dried leaves from the pot, and, yes, talking to my plant. I noticed that after a while, I still had my plant, and after a while, it was even springing new leaves.

This brought my mind to the fact that after we have been through the rigor of unpleasant circumstances, God does the pruning in our lives, such as watering us, putting us in a position to get sunlight, removing the old withered leaves from us, and yes talking with and to us then He gives us new life. He allows us to spring forth new leaves; He gives us a new song to sing, a new attitude toward Him, a new love for others, a new direction, and a new purpose.

There are times in our lives when everything is going well: we have a job and a happy marriage, our children are doing well, and we attend church every week. We are blooming and look as beautiful as the fresh poinsettia plant. Then, disaster strikes, and we lose our house and jobs; children are wayward, and our spouse takes a different direction, and we end up looking like the withered leaves on the plant. BUT GOD kept that tiny spot of green, which gives us hope. Once we keep nurturing that tiny spot of green in our lives with the nutrients of prayer, quality time with God, faith, and spending time in God's word, our hope will be restored, and we will eventually bloom again, just like the first plant.

He promised us in Isaiah 43:19 (KJV), which says, *"Behold, I will do a new thing, now it shall spring forth, shall you not know it? I will even make a way in the wilderness and rivers in the desert."* Let us endeavor to allow God to perform that new thing in our lives and to do the impossible as we continue to make Him the Gardener and Rock of our lives. Be encouraged, hold on, and never let go; once there is life, there is hope. You will rejoice in God for restoring all you have lost and more.

TODAY'S PRAYER

Dear Lord, thank You for being the Author and Artist of our lives. As You perform the duties of pruning on us, let us be receptive and faithful as we receive that new thing You have ordained for us. We claim newness in every aspect of our lives as we say thanks in Jesus' name, Amen.

REFLECTION

What new song is God allowing you to sing now?

___

___

___

___

___

___

___

___

___

___

___

___

___

___

___

DAY SEVENTEEN
FAITH PROVISION

"For he satisfies the thirsty and fills the hungry with good things."

Psalm 107:9 (NIV)

Philippians 4:19 (KJV), *"And my God shall supply all your needs according to his riches in glory by Christ Jesus."* These are the words that kept echoing in my head. After being terminated from my job because I was out sick for over six months and the company could not hold the position for me any longer, I had to take comfort in these words and speak them daily back to God. All my savings had been used up, and I was financially embarrassed. With two kids to support and bills to be paid, we had to be very frugal in our spending and very simple in our living conditions, as my husband was the only breadwinner for the family. It was in no way easy for us, but we decided that we were going to trust in God's Word and we were going to live by faith.

I had dreams that I wanted to fulfill, dreams that if they came through, I would be able to assist my family's needs financially, and dreams that would provide me more time to heal continuously without putting pressure on my body. I shared these dreams with my husband and my girlfriends. It so happened that one of my girlfriends shared one of my dreams in another part of the world. She is trying to get information on her side, and I am trying to get information on my side, but we would share the information with each other. This particular day, she called me, and we were talking about possible outcomes. She also told me that she would have a conversation with another person doing the same thing and would get information about the resources he was using. I told her to share whatever information she got so I could research the same resources even though I had no way of financing it now. She replied to me by saying, 'Listen, girl, this is not about money. We are going to step out in faith and do this thing.' Her comment moved me as it inspired me and reminded me that whatever we ask in Jesus' name in prayer believing, we will receive and also in Ephesians 3:20 (NIV), which says, *"Now to Him who is able to do exceedingly above all that we ask or think according to the power that works within us."*

I prayed and accepted the fact that I would not be able to work outside of home right now and decided that whatever I am doing from home, I will do it well. The next day, I received a message that my brother had sent some money to my account. This money was promised to me for a couple of months now, but God knew that I would need it this time, and so he delayed the process until now. This is money that I can use to get most of the resources that I will need to accomplish one of my dreams, which will allow me to help with the needs of my family and share with others.

God promised us that He will provide for us, He promised that He will take care of us, and He also promised that He will provide people who will help us along the way. He is God all by Himself, He cannot and will not lie and all we have to do is speak back His promises to Him, trust Him and claim these promises. We have to live by faith and not feelings.

TODAY'S PRAYER

Dear Lord, our all-wise Father, we thank You for giving us the wisdom to know that we should trust You. You made Your promises to us, and thank You, O Lord, for keeping them and for providing for us. Help us to live by faith even when we cannot see because You are our Guide, and You will never leave us nor forsake us. In Jesus' name, Amen.

REFLECTION

What are the ways that you would like God to bless you far more than you can imagine?

_____

_____

_____

_____

_____

_____

_____

_____

_____

_____

_____

_____

_____

DAY EIGHTEEN
SUPPORTING MINDS

"Share each other's burdens, and in this way obey the law of Christ."

Galatians 6:2 (NLT)

Our God is awesome! He cannot lie and will not lie. He promised that He would take care of us, and He will do nothing less than take care of us. When the Holy Spirit impressed it on my heart, when we decided, and when my son agreed to be moved to a private school, I was very ill, at home, and was on disability. With the encouragement of a few good people, we finalized the decision. The fee would have been an issue as my husband was the only breadwinner at the time. However, God said it was time for a change, and change it was. After assistance was given and we paid what we could afford, the necessary fees were covered for him to begin classes.

The monthly fees started adding up, and after two months into school, I was terminated from my job because I was out sick for a long period of time, my short-term disability had expired, and I was hospitalized for two weeks. This means total dependence on God. He told us to take no thought for the morrow because the morrow will take care of itself. I am not a person who likes debt, and so, being at home, I decided to use my creative mind to create items that I could use to assist in the payment of the school fee. I organized a fundraising sale at my church, and even though the total was not enough to cover the cost, it was very successful because of the support from the members and visitors who attended the function that was being held. We are very grateful for all the assistance that we have received from others and are happy that they responded when God impressed it on their hearts to support us.

Proverbs 11:25 (NIV) says, *"A generous person will prosper, whoever refreshes others will be refreshed. God has placed everyone on earth to help each other."*

A small act of kindness can actually change a person's life. Helping others glorify God and allow us to not only help someone else to feel good but about themselves, but it helps us to feel good about ourselves. Helping others is a selfless act that makes us happier and healthier.

Hebrews 13:16 (KJV) also encourages us that *"we should not forget to do good and to share, for with such sacrifices God is pleased."* A similar spiritually encouraging verse that can be found in 1 Timothy 6:18 (NIV) reads, *"Command them to do good, to be rich in good deeds, and to be generous and willing to share."* God's ultimate desire is that we would give happily. He doesn't want us to have to give out of obligation. He wants to bless his children. Not so that we can live in complete comfort and luxury but so that we can be even more generous to those around us.

When we are compassionate to others here on earth, we make our Creator happy. God has given us the greatest sacrifice — His only Son. That is a true example of what it means to give. He asks us to make sacrifices to share with our fellowmen. And, when we obey, He will bless us.

TODAY'S PRAYER

Dear Lord, thank You for creating us and for providing an excellent support system for each of us. Please continue to impress it on our hearts to be kind and compassionate here on earth until You come to take us home. Please send Your Holy Spirit to dwell with us. Help us display a daily attitude of gratitude, and please continue to bless us all in Jesus' name. Amen.

REFLECTION

God has created us with a creative mind; what are your creative ways? In what ways can you share with someone in need?

_____

_____

_____

_____

_____

_____

_____

_____

_____

_____

_____

DAY NINETEEN

ONLY A PRAYER REQUEST

"As for me, far be it from me that I should sin against the LORD by failing to pray for you. And I will teach you the way that is good and right."

1 Samuel 12:23 (NIV)

God never ceases to amaze us with His love and His blessings. All He asks us to do is trust Him, and He will provide for us, comfort us, heal us, lead, and direct us. I looked at the check sent to me to assist with my son's school fee, and it was soaked from the teardrops in my eyes. These tears were a mixture of both sadness and joy. It is amazing when I reflect on how God has provided through someone we have never met.

Our Education Sponsor at church decided to ask someone to sponsor my son's school fees. God impressed it on her heart to ask a specific person who sent a check that would cover ninety-five percent of the balance owed. I offered to send a thank you card to the person, but it was advised that the person only wanted us to pray for him or her.

I do not know or do not need to know why the person requested prayer, but it is my duty to petition the throne of grace for that person and everyone that he will impact. My heart is filled with gratitude for this assistance, and I will continue to bless others as much as I can.

God has provided each of us with the ability to assist each other, as no man is an island. In the Garden of Eden, He created Adam and realized that it wasn't a balanced equation, so He created Eve. He created multiple kinds of animals. Each of His creations was created to assist the other. Plants were created to provide food, shelter, clothing, and recreation. He created sunlight to be important to humans, animals, and plants. In Matthew 5:42 (NLT), He admonishes us to *"Give to the one who asks and don't turn away from those who want to borrow."* Jesus never created us to be alone but to live interdependently with each other. God instructed us to pray for each other because He knew that He would answer those prayers. Prayer is the best gift we can offer to others, and we do not have to consider the cost. It is a free gift. We do not have to make an appointment to pray for others, as God is always available to hear and capable of answering our prayers. When we pray for others, it is a way of telling others that we love and care for them. It is also a way of showing others how powerful prayer and our God is.

Paul knew he could not do it alone, and so he asked the brethren in Ephesians 6:18-19 (NIV), "*And pray in the Spirit on all occasions with all kinds of prayers and requests. With this in mind, be alert and always keep on praying for all the Lord's people. Pray also for me that whenever I speak, words may be given to me so that I will fearlessly make known the mystery of the gospel*" to pray for him. Paul was also constantly praying for others. We need the prayers of others to help us get through the daily walk of life. When we pray for others, there is a ripple effect as not only the receiver but the giver and their descendants are blessed.

Let us continue to bless others with the blessings that God has given us.

TODAY'S PRAYER

Dear Lord, thank You so much for showing up and proving Your promises daily. Lord, even though You are our Creator, You also call us friend. Help us to build a relationship with You as we continue to trust in Your promises to us. Thanks for impressionable hearts. We pray in Jesus' name, Amen.

REFLECTION

How has God provided for you through a stranger lately?

_____

_____

_____

_____

_____

_____

_____

_____

_____

_____

_____

_____

_____

DAY TWENTY

THE POWER SOURCE

"He gives strength to the weary, and to him who lacks might He increases power."

Isaiah 40:29 (NASB)

The words in the book 'Whisper' by Mark Batterson danced squarely in my mind. They were so profound that I found it very hard to be distracted. My daughter sat beside me, watching her iPad, which was plugged in due to very low battery life. I placed her at a specific location that would allow the charger to be connected to the device. She kept moving further away from the location, which made it difficult for the charger to fit comfortably into the device. In a matter of time, I watched her shift further away until she unplugged the device in frustration. I plugged in the charger and explained again to her that for her to watch the program, she had to stay in that location so the device could be plugged into the charger, which would increase the battery life, and she could continue to watch her program. Without that process, the battery will die shortly.

I thought carefully about our spiritual lives.

We have to place ourselves in a position where we can be connected to God so we can live on earth and live eternally with Him when He comes back the second time. If we are not connected to Him through prayer, Bible studies, community service, and talking daily with Him, then we will lose connection, and the further we go from that Source, the weaker we become. We have to feast our minds, our hearts, our mouths, our calling, our choices, our eyes, our hands, our bodies, and our feet on the word of God, as well as on things that are in accordance with God's will. We can only accomplish these and fixate our minds on heavenly things through the help of Christ. He comforts us through His words in Psalm 145:18(NASB), *"The Lord is near to all who call on Him, to all who call on Him in truth."*

He also reminds us that we should be sober and of a sound mind. God is our Source for everything you could ever need or want. By coming to Jesus every day, you draw from the Source of all resources. He is the love you so need, the joy that will motivate and renew you, and the strength that will carry you through the day, no matter how much supply you require. God never runs out of more for His children. Christ wants to be the Power Source in us so that we can do all things. But to experience the transformation of that great power, we need to be "plugged into" Christ as our Source. *"God has spoken plainly, and I have heard it many times: Power, O God, belongs to you."* Psalm 62:11 (NLT). Without this Source, we are weak and powerless, confused, have no sense of direction, and our vision becomes blurry.

It is very important that we begin our days and our mornings by plugging into the Power Source. Jesus said it like this (John 15:4-5, 7), *"Abide in Me, and I in you. As the branch cannot bear fruit of itself, unless it abides in the vine, neither can you, unless you abide in Me. I am the vine, you are the branches. He who abides in Me, and I in him, bears much fruit; for without Me you can do nothing... If you abide in Me, and My words abide in you..."*

When we develop a daily experience of tapping into our Source of Power, we will be energized to live a life of faith and purpose.

TODAY'S PRAYER

Dear Lord, thank You for being our Source of Life. Please help us to stay connected to You every second of the day. Keep our minds stayed on You always, help us to be desperate for the Source of power, so we can be transformed by You. In Jesus's name, AMEN.

REFLECTION

When and why was the last time that you had to get reconnected to the "Power Source?"

_____

_____

_____

_____

_____

_____

_____

_____

_____

_____

_____

_____

_____

DAY TWENTY ONE
PERSONALLY KNOWN

"You saw me before I was born. Every day of my life was recorded in your book. Every moment was laid out before a single day had passed."

Psalm 139:16 (NLT)

Taking a trip to the Emergency Room is not my favorite Friday afternoon activity, but I was forced to do it as my son was in pain. We sat patiently in the emergency room, waiting to be seen by the Doctor. The Emergency Medical Services (EMS) entered the right entrance with a young man on a stretcher, and shortly after, a lady and her husband entered the left entrance. Their eyes were glued to the young man on the stretcher as they tried to scrutinize every movement made. I was impressed to speak with them as I asked if the young man was their son and to encourage them that I would pray for him and that he would be fine. I asked his name so I could be a little personal, as I mentioned his name in my prayer.

Sometime after getting the young man settled in the room and being seen by the Doctor, the lady and her husband stepped out of the room again. By this time, my son was asleep. The lady enquired about my son and offered the same advice, saying she would pray for him. She also asked me what his name was. Her eyes lit up as she said, 'Funny enough that I have his name written in my hand' as she turned her hand to show me. When I looked, indeed, two letters TY etched in her handwritten in blue ink. I know that was only God Himself.

My friend, that was an amazing thing, but the most important thing is found in Jeremiah 1:5 (KJV), which states, *"Before I formed thee in the belly, I knew thee."* We are so special to God that He has created us, and then He redeemed us; He has called us by our name because we are His. Isaiah 43:1 (NIV) reminds us that we should *"fear not, God has redeemed us, He has called us by our name, and we are His."* It is such a wonderful feeling when we are called by our names. It shows that someone knows us. This scripture explains to us that God gets personal with us. More than knowing our names, God knows our framework. He formed us; He knows our strengths and our weaknesses. He knows our pains and our joys. He knows our inside and our outside. Each detail in our lives matters to God, whether big or small. Just as God knows us personally, His desire for us is that we should get to know Him personally too. Not just to know of Him but to spend time with Him daily so we can build a closer relationship with Him to know Him better. He wants us to be able to say, 'I know His name, call Him by name, He is my Savior, He is my Redeemer, and He is my Lord.' God delights when we truly know Him, love Him, and enjoy the blessings of His faithful love, grace, mercy, and righteousness. Do you long to know God? Is He the desire of your heart? Do you want to have that one permanent God-relationship? Then reach out to Him, seek after Him, and pursue Him. Those who seek Him will find Him.

TODAY'S PRAYER

Dear Lord, we thank You for knowing us before You formed us in our mother's womb. We adore You for fearfully and wonderfully creating us. God, we are amazed at how even the very hair on our head is numbered, and You are not confused with my numbers as opposed to someone else's. Thank You for creating us and redeeming us. Direct us as we seek to know You personally. We thank You for Your love. Amen.

REFLECTION

How do you feel to know that God knows you personally?

_____
_____
_____
_____
_____
_____
_____
_____
_____
_____
_____
_____
_____

DAY TWENTY TWO

TRUST IN GOD

"But when you ask him, be sure that your faith is in God alone. Do not waver, for a person with divided loyalty is as unsettled as a wave of the sea that is blown and tossed by the wind."

James 1:6 (NLT)

Promises are kept, promises are unkept, expectations and apologies follow suit, and the cycle starts over. Human beings are very famous for making promises and having expectations of others. Some people develop anxiety when promises are made to them. Years gone by, if and when a promise was made to me, I would be anxious for the time to mature, or I couldn't wait to see what was promised to me. Then, I would be so disappointed when things didn't materialize. I have reached the point now where I do not appreciate or accept any promises from anyone. I try to have fewer expectations of others; if I do, they are simple, realistic expectations. It has been proven to me for quite some time that most times when we have expectations, they bring disappointments, disappointments bring hurt, and hurt brings sadness. No one wants to live a sad or hurtful life, but this is what life throws at us in some unlearned cases. The songwriter penned the words of a song, *'Stand up, stand up for Jesus, stand in His strength alone. The arm of flesh will fail you; ye dare not trust your own.'*

Micah 7:5 (KJV) says, *"Do not trust in a friend, do not put your confidence in a companion, guard the doors of your mouth from her who lies in your bosom."* This is because we were shaped in iniquity, and our mothers conceived us in sin. Men are not faithful, dishonest, subject to change and failure, and can easily forget their promises.

Thank God there is hope, hope that we can find in promises given to us in the Bible found in Romans 4:21(NLT), *"He was fully convinced that God is able to do what he promises."*

God is not a man that He should lie. God cannot change, He will not forget His promises, He cannot lie and He's faithful to the end. All we have to do is trust Him as He is our ultimate Source of help. He is God and cannot change.

"*Some trust in chariots and some in horses, but we trust in the name of the LORD our God. They are brought to their knees and fall, but we rise up and stand firm.*" Psalm 20:7-8 (KJV). God shows us that we can trust Him through His character. He is loyal to us and faithful in His promises. We can trust God on a good or a bad day, and the result will be the same – Faithful God. Do you only trust God on good days? It's easy to trust God when things are going well, but we must believe in Him at all times. He will be there for us through it all. Trusting God is a Priority and should never be an option.

TODAY'S PRAYER

Dear Lord, thank You for Your promises, which bring hope and assurance to us daily. Please help us to trust in You, who is our Source of help, You are faithful and cannot change. Please help us to try to be more like You, which will help us to decrease disappointments for ourselves and others. Keep us in Your love, and continue to bless us immeasurably. I pray in Jesus' name, Amen.

REFLECTION

How do you feel when faced with unbroken promises? What are some promises from the Bible that you use for comfort?

_____

_____

_____

_____

_____

_____

_____

_____

_____

_____

_____

_____

DAY TWENTY THREE
FOLLOW THE WAY

"Then spake Jesus again unto them, saying, I am the light of the world: he that followeth me shall not walk in darkness, but shall have the light of life."

John 8:12 (KJV)

'Ensure that you follow me closely' were the instructions given by my husband. Rewind a few weeks prior to this specific instruction. My husband drives over two and a half hours one way to and from work daily. The trusted van that we had decided on was tired and needed to rest approximately two days before my husband would take six weeks of medical leave from work due to a major surgery he had scheduled. He had the van towed to a mechanic in the neighborhood and made plans for them to hold it there until it was closer to his return-to-work date and after a fair recovery period.

We drove over together a week before he returned to work, and then I would follow him back home.

I listened carefully to his instructions and warned our daughter to either take a nap or enjoy the scenery, as I did not want to be distracted. Due to the fact that my husband was on familiar turf and knew his way due to his daily experience of taking this route, I never even entertained the fact of putting the destination in the GPS. So, we started our journey.

For every turn my husband turned, I turned also. For every brake light I noticed on the van, I did the same. For every stop he came to, I followed suit. I trusted my husband, and he took us home safely with concise driving directions. But how many times do we follow the GPS or follow someone who is driving, and we still get lost?

My friend, we have the privilege of having a Father who not only knows the way but also knows who is the way. The Bible tells us in John 14: 6 (NIV), *"I am the way, the truth and the life. No one comes to the Father but through me."*

In these words, Jesus explained to us that He is the only way to Heaven. The only true measure of righteousness and the definite source of our spiritual life. There is no other path to Heaven but by following Him. *"Salvation is found in no other name under heaven given to men by which we are saved."* Acts 4:12 (KJV)

Jesus offers us His own GPS, the Bible, in which directions are very clear as to how to put self aside and to follow Him directly. This GPS will not only lead us on the correct path on earth but will, most importantly, lead us to our eternal home as it is connected to the true WAY. Let us trust His route as He is the way. Following Jesus means to strive to be like Him and to make Him Lord of our lives. Let us invite others to follow Him also, as He is the way, the truth, and the life.

TODAY'S PRAYER

Dear Heavenly Father, we thank You for being our Creator. We praise You for Your continued direction, and we honor You for being patient with us and for leading us on the right path when we go astray. Please help us to trust and follow You with confidence that we will never get lost with You. At any time that we stray from Your leading, please give us a right about turn back to Your guiding hands. I pray and say thanks, in Jesus' name. Amen.

REFLECTION

Describe a scenario when you had to follow an instruction given by the Holy Spirit.

_____

_____

_____

_____

_____

_____

_____

_____

_____

_____

_____

DAY TWENTY-FOUR
THE REAL ONE PROVIDED

"If ye then, being evil, know how to give good gifts unto your children, how much more shall your Father which is in heaven give good things to them that ask him?"

Matthew 7:11 (KJV)

Singing, playing musical instruments, and dancing are activities that keep my daughter happy and engaged. She uses real instruments as well as pretend instruments. One Friday night after family worship, she took her toy shovel, which she refers to as her digger, and my son's pointer and started playing and humming. My husband was so shocked at what she was doing that he called me quickly to look at the actions of our daughter. I was amazed when I looked at her; she was playing the violin with her toys. I took my phone and started recording her. I noticed that even though we don't have a violin present in the house and there is no role model of a violinist, she was humming the exact pitch of a violin, her fingers were moving according to the notes on each string, and the bow was moving rhythmically on her pretend violin. At the end of her show, she said, 'I play my violin.' Without hesitation, I started researching the price of violins. I shared the video with some of my family members and friends who too were amazed of her knowledge and action.

The next day, I checked my phone only to receive a message from a very special friend of mine to say that she would gift my daughter a real violin. I was dumbstruck, silenced, teary-eyed, happy, thankful, and grateful all at the same time. I begged her not to let me cry as I was confused with all the emotions bottled inside of me due to how God is amazingly awesome to us. She explained that her daughter had gotten two, but the one she would gift to my daughter had never been out of the box, and she has outgrown using that small one. The statement that had me in awe was when she said her daughter wanted to give it to another person the day before I sent the video, but they weren't sure if the person had an interest, so they wanted to gift it to her.

God knows exactly who to bless with what at the appropriate time. He inspires the correct hearts at the most appropriate time. Matthew 7:11 (KJV) states, *"If ye then, being evil, know how to give good gifts unto your children, how much more shall your Father which is in heaven give good things to them."* God always has our best interest at heart. And He is all-knowing. He will only give us things that are *good* for us. The greatest gift we've ever been given was not bought in a store. No cash was exchanged. It was not even wrapped. Yet it cost the Gift Giver everything. The Bible says in John 3:*17 (KJV), "God sent not his son into the world to condemn the world but that the world through Him might be saved."*

This is the greatest gift ever. He came to Earth to die—so that we could be made right with God. God gave us a free gift of salvation when Jesus took our sins upon himself. But it's a gift we must receive. The Bible says, *"Yet to all who did receive him, to those who believed in his name, he gave the right to become children of God."* John 1:12 (NIV).

How can we not love Him for blessing us over and over again? How can we not share our blessings? How can we not express attitudes of gratitude daily? Let us build that close connection with Him so He can continue to bless us, and we can hear and listen to Him when He tells us to share with others.

TODAY'S PRAYER

Dear Lord, please cleanse us from all iniquities. Lord, please renew us in You. Great Redeemer, thank You for blessing us over and over again. Thank You for the greatest gift ever. Please help us to continue to share our blessings with others. Connect us with You so we will be a living testimony for You. Show us how to bless others as we wait on You patiently and say thanks. In Jesus' name, Amen.

REFLECTION

Do you like to give or receive gifts?

_____
_____
_____
_____
_____
_____
_____
_____
_____
_____
_____

DAY TWENTY FIVE
MUSICAL WIND

"For ever since the world was created, people have seen the earth and sky. Through everything God made, they can clearly see his invisible qualities—his eternal power and divine nature. So they have no excuse for not knowing God."

Romans 1:20 (NLT)

I sat staring outside through the window. I was mesmerized by the dance moves the trees were making as the musical notes played heavily around them by the wind. I was amazed by just looking carefully in every direction, trying to see if I could see the specific object called the wind. I look during the days, and I see the sun, and at night, I see the moon. However, while searching high and low, I could not find the wind, but I could see the effects of the action.

I pondered and associated this with Jesus; we cannot literally see Him, but we know He is with us by His amazing actions towards us. The wind was not blowing in my specific location solely based on the weather report. It was active in multiple states, possibly countries, at the same time.

John 3:8 (NLT) states, *"The wind blows wherever it wants. Just as you can hear the wind but can't tell where it comes from or where it is going, so you can't explain how people are born of the Spirit."*

The wind is powerful, the results can be seen and felt, it is invisible, and it goes wherever it wishes to go. We just cannot physically touch it. These characteristics of the wind are also true of the Holy Spirit. The Holy Spirit is powerful; we cannot see the Holy Spirit, but we can see the results of His work, and He is omnipresent. Listening to a sermon, I learned that the Hebrew word 'ruach' means spirit, breath, and wind, depending on the context in which it is used. I went searching with my inquiring mind and found out that Ruach HaKodesh, which appears in

Psalm 51:11 (KJV), *"Cast me not away from thy presence; and take not thy holy spirit from me,"* is the Hebrew word for the Holy Spirit.

Our omnipotent God does not work in a single location, a single life, or a single family at any given time. If you take a survey, you will find numerous people giving their experiences of what God did for them at that specific time. It also dawned on me that in all of God's creation, human beings are the only ones that have a dependence on the other created elements. The sun, moon, and stars shine without any human action. The plants grow and thrive with nutrients from the rain and from the sun.

However, human beings depend on the plants, animals, sun, wind and rain for fresh air, vitamins, food, clothing and shelter. How is the Holy Spirit moving in your life like the wind today? God is encouraging us today through His *ruach*. Let us allow Him to move in us, as we continue to aspire to be renewed each day through His power.

God emphasizes in His words that the birds and fowls of the air have enough to eat, and He will always provide for us. How magnificent is our God!

TODAY'S PRAYER

Dear God, our Creator, and Savior, thank You for creating us as well as the other elements that You knew we would need. Lord, it is amazing looking at Your creation. The uniqueness of Your creation allows us to see a fraction of how wise You are. Thank You for blessing us over and over again. Forgive us for taking Your creation for granted. Help us to appreciate Your creation as we adore Your matchless name, in Jesus' name, Amen.

REFLECTION

How important is nature to your life?

_____

_____

_____

_____

_____

_____

_____

_____

_____

_____

_____

_____

DAY TWENTY SIX

TINY STEPS

"For I can do everything through Christ, who gives me strength."

Philippians 4:13 (NLT)

One day, I started note-taking in a fairly new binder on binder leaves. I was very uncomfortable each time I was expected to write on the back of each leaf because there wasn't enough cushion to write on a smooth section. I persisted through the discomfort, hoping to take enough notes to allow me enough pages on the back side of the leaf to write smoothly. Each completed page was enough to get closer to the goal of completing my course as well as writing comfortably.

I spoke with a girlfriend who told me about her journey of taking little steps. I encouraged her by informing her that the little steps that we take eventually become our journey. A few days later, I received an email that basically explained a lady who had taken up climbing the mountains. On her journey, there were challenges, and she was very anxious to reach the top, which she did, and the view was amazing. Later on that day, I was doing some reading, and I stumbled across a quote with the same message, 'taking tiny steps will allow you to fulfill a dream.' As a believer in Christ, I believe that an intimate relationship with God is available to every believer, but it must be cultivated, nurtured, and developed like any other relationship. A child grows daily and develops into different psychological, physical, social, or mental stages as he or she grows and gets older. This is the same effect as that of a believer in Christ. We take our little steps, and then they become our journey as we develop a relationship with our Maker. God desires to have an intimate relationship with us and fellowship with us on a daily basis. In Revelation 3:20 (KJV), Jesus says, *"Behold, I stand at the door, and knock: if any man hear my voice, and open the door, I will come in to him, and will sup with him, and he with me."* The word sup in this verse carries the idea of fellowship. Jesus is saying that He wants to fellowship with us.

A famous quote states that 'Rome wasn't built in a day.' There are things that we can do, should do, or need to do in order for us to grow. We can only accomplish these things if we depend on God to lead us, take a leap of faith, and take tiny steps. If we do not start, we will not be able to finish. Upon completion, we will always feel fulfilled because we would have done something out of our comfort zone. The Bible tells us in Philippians 4:13(NLT), *"I can do everything through Christ who gives me strength."* He is waiting for us to take that first step. His hands are outstretched, and He is waiting patiently for us to put ours in His. Why don't you take the opportunity to allow Him to lead and guide you? There are opportunities waiting for us to grow, whether spiritually or socially, but we have to take the initial step.

TODAY'S PRAYER

Thank You, God, for giving us wisdom. Lord, please continue to hold on to us and lead us in the pathway You have ordained for us. Help us to meditate on how You have led us in the past, how You are leading us now, and how You will continue to lead us. Help us to not have You waiting with outstretched arms without us placing our hands into Yours as we're confident that Your directions are best for us. In Jesus name, Amen.

REFLECTION

What tiny steps are you taking now that you are confident will become your journey?

_____

_____

_____

_____

_____

_____

_____

_____

_____

_____

_____

DAY TWENTY SEVEN
A PREPARED WAY

"He is your glory and He is your God, who has done these great and awesome things for you which your eyes have seen."

Habakkuk 1:5 (NIV)

I jumped out of bed at the buzzing of my phone to see my husband's phone number displayed on my phone screen. I quickly answered before he disconnected the call due to the fact that it had been ringing for a while. On the other end of the phone, he explained that he had some challenges driving to work as it seemed as if the car battery was dying. We briefly discussed the topic and possible solutions and then ended the call. A couple of hours later, he called to inform me that a gentleman at his job who is a part-time mechanic discovered that the alternator had died. He purchased the needed part and had it installed.

God kept the alternator alive until he reached work, where he knew that the person was present and was able to correct the problem. God provides everything we have and need as the Creator of our life. It is very reassuring to know that in the midst of our challenging times, God has a plan for us, and it is always the best one. He told us in Psalm 37:23 (NASB) that "*the steps of a man are established by the Lord, and He delights in his way.*" In Romans 8:28 (NIV), the Bible tells us, *"And we know that for those who love God all things work together for good, for those who are called according to his purpose."*

God's plan for us is revealed a little at a time as we follow Him, and His plan may look different at different sections of our journey with Him. His ways are higher than ours Isaiah 55:8–9, and His timing is beyond our comprehension. He may even use delays or redirections to refine our desires and strengthen our faith in Him. As we wait for God to answer our requests, we can trust that His timing is always perfect.

God knows the beginning from the end, and so when our lives are placed in His hands, we don't have to worry about the future because He holds the future in His hands. He cares about all the details of our lives, whether we classify them as big or small. He is our Waymaker, and His trail is perfectly organized for us; we just have to walk in the imprint of the footprints that He placed before us. If you've ever felt lost or uncertain about your path, worry no more. No matter the situation you may be facing right now, you can find solace in the knowledge that God is your Waymaker and He will open new doors for you just as He had promised.

TODAY'S PRAYER

Dear Lord, thank You for holding our future in Your hands. We adore You for being concerned about the tiny details of our lives and providing a way out even before we think about it. Help us to trust Your plans for us. In Jesus' name, Amen.

REFLECTION

What is your reaction when something works out in your favor, and you are confident that it happened that way because you trusted God?

_____
_____
_____
_____
_____
_____
_____
_____
_____
_____
_____
_____
_____
_____

DAY TWENTY EIGHT
FAITHFUL PROMISES

"Every good and perfect gift is from above, coming down from the Father of the heavenly lights, who does not change like shifting shadows."

James 1:17 (NIV)

One day, I awoke very early in the morning to the music the birds were playing outside. The tune was melodious, the pitch was perfect, and the rhythm was constant. What a privilege it is to be awoken by nature, not the regular sound of cars or sirens. I ventured into a new hobby, gardening, and so recently, I have tried to wake up before everyone else just to walk outside to water my vegetables and my flowers, talk with them, and see their progress. But most of all, I want to talk with my Creator and enjoy nature. After doing my plant exercises, I stood under the big tree in the backyard and asked the question, 'God, where is it that you want us to go.'

My husband and I have been praying again about relocating and unlike the previous times when we were intrigued by what we saw briefly whether by short visits or research, and God said, 'no, wrong direction. ' Even thinking about it now there was one specific state that we chose one location and we got an offer for a different location but the answer was still no. So, this time we would have to take a different approach. And so, we would rather have Him choose for us.

Before I went outside, I sent my girlfriend a message highlighting that innocent children are innocent, and sometimes, it would be better for us to take that approach and leave our burdens at Jesus' feet. After my moment outside, I came inside the house, checked my phone, and noticed that my girlfriend sent me her devotional for the day, which highlighted the same topic I just texted her about, as well as the scripture Matthew 7:11 (KJV) which says, *"If ye being evil, know how to give good gifts to your children, how much more shall your Father which is in heaven give good gifts to them that ask him."*

Then she shared with me another devotional that her friend shared with her, which highlighted the scripture passage in James 1:17 (NLT), which reads, *"Whatever is good and perfect is a gift coming down to us from God our Father, who created all the lights in the heavens. He never changes or casts a shifting shadow."*

Jesus gave me these promises this morning to remind me, my family, and us all that He has the perfect gift for us. Our duty is to trust Him and to follow His directives.

His promises are given to all of us to claim. He has good and perfect gifts for everyone. Are you looking to move to a new location, trying to get a new job, or just taking a different step or making a different move?

Read God's promises back to Him, make your requests known unto Him in prayer and supplication, claim His promises, wait on Him, and be obedient to His leading. He will give you the desires of your heart as long as it is in accordance with His will. Just trust Him.

TODAY'S PRAYER

Dear Lord, thank You so much for Your Holy Spirit. Thank You for giving us Your promises and helping us to understand that we have not because we ask not. Help us to be humble in our asking and confident in our receiving. Help us to be obedient to Your words and to trust in You while we wait patiently for Your leading. Give us a discerning spirit; we pray and say thanks. In Jesus' name, Amen.

REFLECTION

What promise are you claiming at this time?

_____

_____

_____

_____

_____

_____

_____

_____

_____

_____

DAY TWENTY NINE
REAPING THE HARVEST

"So neither the one who plants nor the one who waters is anything, but only God, who makes things grow. The one who plants and the one who waters have one purpose, and they will each be rewarded according to their own labor.

1 Corinthians 3:7-8 (NIV)

'Oh no! One more bad one', I exclaimed upon discovering a spoiled tomato in the refrigerator. My daughter and I were in a planting season, so I decided not to waste it but to see what we could get from it. We squeezed the tomato seeds into a pot with soil. This activity was fun for her as she showed how strong she was in squeezing the tomato. After a short waiting period, we were able to transplant the little plants into the soil. We chose the best location as we wanted to ensure that the plants would get enough sunlight and water from the raindrops as well as the best soil type. It was such an activity, and we were responsible for watering the plants every morning. When the plants reached a certain height, we used pantyhose to tie them to wire props, as this would serve as support for the tiny stalks. We watched in excitement daily and cared for them as we did ourselves.

Then came the day when we noticed blooms showing up, and then balls started popping up on the stalks. We counted one tomato, two tomatoes, and three tomatoes until we stopped at twenty-five tomatoes. Big, medium, and small tomatoes were there from that one tomato fruit we squeezed so hard into a pot. The most exciting part came when we were able to walk to the backyard, pick tomatoes from the trees, eat them, and share them. My husband expressed that the taste was different from that of a regular tomato from the food store. Enjoying the labor of our hands indeed. Harvest period.

I reflected on the many seasons of life we have to go through, the many journeys we would have to embark upon, the different roads we have to tread, and the many waiting periods we have experienced. There are even times when we think that we are too sinful and that we are no good. I assure you that just as we were able to harvest so many good tomatoes from one bad one, God is willing and able to cleanse us from all unrighteousness and turn our mess into a message. He is able to transform us from bad to good. Our duty is to confess our sins sincerely to Him, to ask Him to change us, and to allow Him to work in us. When He transforms us, we look differently, act differently, walk differently, and even talk differently. There is a change in us. 2 Corinthians 5:17 (NKJV) tells us, *"Therefore if any man be in Christ, he is a new creature: old things are passed away; behold, all things are become new."*

Are you in a waiting period? Are you in an uncomfortable season? Are you walking on rugged terrain?

Just like the process of planting through to the harvesting season of the tomatoes, Jesus, the Alpha and the Omega, the Beginning and the End, knows our every moment. He is the one who created us, thus knowing everything about our lives from start to finish. We need all the squeezing we need, the type of soil we need, the amount of soil to place us in, the specific location at the appropriate time, and the support we need to help us through life. When we are faithful to Him, trusting Him totally, then He will pour on us a blessing that we will not have enough room to receive. He will bless us in ways that we could not see how; He will amaze us and blow our minds at the wonders of His hands. As we continue to live, let us allow God to continue to be our Chief Farmer as we patiently await the harvesting season.

TODAY'S PRAYER

Dear Lord, please forgive us for the sins we have committed. Help us to hate sin so we can strive for holiness. We adore You for being our perfect example. We ask that You will help us to allow You to be our Planter as we wait patiently to reap the best harvest. Help us to trust You as we wait. In Jesus' name, Amen.

REFLECTION

What season are you in, and what harvest are you anticipating reaping?

_____
_____
_____
_____
_____
_____
_____
_____
_____
_____
_____
_____
_____

DAY THIRTY

COVERED BY AN ANGEL

" For he shall give his angels charge over thee, to keep thee in all thy ways."

Psalm 91:11 (KJV)

GET DOWN!!! GET DOWN!!! EVERYBODY GET DOWN!!! The voice shouted as explosions could be heard approximately ten feet away. We were newlyweds, and my husband decided that he would be the one to move from his location as a job was awaiting him. He had applied for a dream job, was hired, and was excited to begin working. I decided to take the Greyhound bus to visit him as well as to help him with the things he was taking with him. Unfortunately, there was a three-hour layover at a particular bus station. Whenever I am traveling, I have to give a roving report to my family members and friends as to the specific location that I am at. As soon as I stepped off the bus and into the bus station, I called my husband to give him my update, and then I called one of my friends to give my report and pass the time by. I noticed about three well-dressed men walking from one end of the station to the other. There was something about them, but I could not pinpoint what it was.

GET DOWN!!!! GET DOWN!!! EVERYBODY GET DOWN!!! The voice shouted as gunshots echoed in the building, and people were running and getting down on the floor as they were commanded to. My girlfriend started screaming and crying for help even though she was in another country and could offer no help, or so I thought at the moment. She managed to run to another girlfriend's house as she was in shock and didn't know what to do. They were on one phone praying with me, I was on the other end of the line crying and praying, and the other phone was used to contact and inform my husband about the situation.

People were injured, and a policeman and the suspect were dead approximately ten feet away from me. The swat team was sweeping the building, FBI members were investigating, reporters were reporting the news, sirens were wailing, people, including myself, were still crying, and the dogs were sniffing everyone. I was and is still traumatized.

Before I fell to the ground, the Lord knew what would happen and sent His angels to cover me. The Bible tells me in Psalm 34:7 (KJV) that *"the angel of the Lord encampeth round about them that fear him and delivereth them."* God knew what was going to happen long before it happened. He knew I would need comfort, so He allowed me to be on the phone with my friend to have that support. Are you scared, are you frustrated, or are you disappointed? Are you in a situation where you need support or help? Trust in God, and call on Him to help you. He promised, *"He will give His angels charge concerning you, to guard you in all your ways."* Psalm 91:11 (NASB). He says what He means, and He means what He says. He is faithful to His promises. Being under God's care provides us incredible strength and comfort in every battle we face. God's covering protection and love helps us to understand that we are held secure by a Mighty God.

TODAY'S PRAYER

Dear Lord, our Shield and Defender. We ask that You will hide us under the shadow of the Almighty. Wash us and make us clean, O Lord. Our righteousness is like filthy rags, so please wash us and make us whiter than snow. Thank You for being our help in times of trouble. Thank You for sending Your angels to protect us, our family, and friends to support and love us. Help us to trust You with our lives, as You are always fighting for us. You want to save us so that we can live eternally with You. We bless Your name and praise You in Jesus' name, Amen.

REFLECTION

Are you scared, frustrated, or disappointed? Are you in a situation where you need support or help?

_____

_____

_____

_____

_____

_____

_____

_____

_____

_____

DAY THIRTY ONE
NEVER TOO BUSY

"Ask and it will be given to you; seek and you will find; knock and the door will be opened to you. For everyone who asks receives; the one who seeks finds; and to the one who knocks, the door will be opened."

Matthew 7:7-8 (NIV)

We sat quietly at the table, ready to devour our delicious meal. Our plates were beautifully decorated with the colors yellow, green, orange, red, and white, all positioned in a creative design. 'We eat with our eyes first' is a true statement, as what we see helps us quickly determine whether we are going to enjoy this meal. We graced the table and started to eat.

At every bite, my toddler daughter said the word 'yummy' with expression and requested that we do the same. There is no doubt we enjoyed our meal. She then jumped from the table and walked over to the fridge. When asked where she was going, she responded that she was going to talk with Jesus. Her dad and I both looked at each other questioningly. Then we heard her say, 'Jesus, You want to have a picnic with us?' And continued with another phrase.

It surprised us to hear her inviting Jesus to come dine with us. After all, we prayed and thanked Him for the food and asked for nutritional values to be added to our bodies, but we never asked Him to join us. There was a profound lesson for us in that question that our daughter asked. We pondered on her actions and asked God to help us to continue to do what we were admonished in Proverbs 22:6 (NASB) to do, which says, *"Train up a child in the way he should go, even when he is old he will not depart from it."*

Sometimes, we find ourselves so busy with the hustle and bustle of our daily activities. Jesus is never too busy to spend time with each of us as we are all the apple of His eyes. When we call on Jesus, there is never a busy signal, or please leave your message at the beep. There is never a do not disturb sign on His door, a poor connection, or a dropped Wi-Fi signal. He is omnipotent, omniscient, and omnipresent. He is willing, ready, and waiting patiently for us to give Him an invitation.

Have you ever asked Jesus to join you at your 'picnic'? Whatever your picnic is, be it your job, your travels, your visit to the church, your conversations, your schools, your worship moments, your game night, or even when shopping, do you invite Him? Jesus is waiting to join us for all our picnic moments. He is not only waiting for our invitation, but He invites Himself; all we have to do is accept Him at our picnic table.

The Bible tells us in Matthew 19:14 (NIV) that *Jesus said, "Let the little children come to me, and do not hinder them, for the kingdom of heaven belongs to such as these."* Children hold a special place in Jesus' heart. We are all God's children, and we hold that special place.

Let us take that moment today to send Him that invite, and I can assure you that we will enjoy our meal in the presence of the Holy One. Jesus also sends us an invite as He welcomes us to His banqueting table. His banner over us is love.

We should humble ourselves and call on Jesus at any time. We should be still to hear Him respond, and we should be aware that He wants to be always with us.

TODAY'S PRAYER

Dear Lord, we thank You for the lessons that You teach us through our children. We ask that You give us humility so that we can invite You into our presence as You want to spend all the time with us. Thank You for being omnipresent and never being too busy for us. Please help us accept Your invitation to be with You always as You invite us to sit at Your welcome table and feast with You forever in Your Heavenly Kingdom. We praise You in Jesus' name, Amen.

REFLECTION

Do you find yourself too busy for God? How can you reorganize your schedule to spend more time with God?

_____

_____

_____

_____

_____

_____

_____

_____

_____

_____

_____

DAY THIRTY TWO
TRUSTING THROUGH THE RUGGED TERRAIN

"Behold, God is my salvation, I will trust and not be afraid; For the LORD GOD is my strength and song, And He has become my salvation."

Isaiah 12:2 (NASB)

Sometimes we are up, sometimes down. Sometimes happy, sometimes sad. It's not an easy road on this journey. I travel this journey with my eyes wide open, but it sometimes surprises me. I can recall as far back as three years old when I questioned my grandma about an unpleasant situation that included me. She tried her best to clarify the information, and I was comfortable with the answer that she gave me at the time, explaining that whatever happens in life, God is always with me.

Traveling this journey called life, I refer to it as my 'rugged terrain.' I ventured with my eyes wide open, but sometimes it took me by surprise. I started out smoothly and thought everything would continue on the same path, but I ended up on a rocky path. I wondered if I was heading in the right direction but confirmed shortly that it was. On that path, I bumped into unkind friends and unpleasant family members. I managed to push my way through with the kindness of others and use those rocks to motivate me to continue on my journey. I was back on a smooth path now where I was being successful in the earthly form. Then, all of a sudden, I bumped into an unexpected object called illness and fell over a cliff. Staying in the valley through aches and pains for a couple of days, months, and even years, I managed to climb my way out as if I were practicing rock climbing. I made three steps forward with love, care, and support, then fell five steps down with doubt. I pushed forward with prayer and was limping my way through with the promises that I learned to lean on. I was very tired from climbing and stopped to take a rest at the top of the hill. I had to drink from the well called the Bible even while I was resting. I think now I have enough strength to continue my journey. So I headed out again. I smiled as I stepped on the smooth path again. This feeling would have encouraged me to reach my destination quicker, but as I looked ahead, I realized I had a far way to go. I tried to see as far as I could but could only see a short distance, and it looked totally different from the image I had in my mind. I continued my journey as I sang and worshipped. After a while, I knew that I would hit another obstacle due to circumstances, but I could not identify when and what it would be. Suddenly, I felt it, yes, termination of a job it was. Faith and patience quickly ended that phase of the journey. I was taught as a young child that if, at first, I fail, I try and try again until I succeed, so I would not turn back, and I would continue my journey. It is easier to continue than to turn back and have to start over, so I continued with total dependence. I also learned that each obstacle would help me to prepare for the next challenge. I struggled through the hills of losing loved ones, fighting through tears of sadness, rejection, mental abuse, and failures. But continued my journey with trust and prayer. I still have a long way to go, but I will continue because I know that I am traveling with Jesus, who is my Master GPS and who is knowledgeable about my entire journey. The promise is given to us in Joshua 1:9 (KJV), which says, *"Have I not commanded you? Be strong and courageous. Do not be afraid; do not be discouraged, for the Lord your God will be with you wherever you go."*

You may be traveling the journey of your rugged terrain. The GPS is prepared for us; our Waymaker knows the position of all our bumps, rocks, hills, and mountains, and He promises that He will always be with us. He has been with us at the start of our journey, the middle, and the ending. He will never leave us alone. Isaiah 43:2 (NLT) tells us, *"When you go through deep waters, I will be with you. When you go through rivers of difficulty, you will not drown. When you walk through the fire of oppression, you will not be burned up, the flames will not consume you."*

Whatever our situation is, whatever position we're in, whether we are on the bumps, in the valley, or on the mountaintop, take courage that Jesus is with us and He is carrying us through. All we have to do is to trust Him through our rugged terrain.

TODAY'S PRAYER

Dear Jesus, thank You for the experiences we have while traveling. We love You for being with us every step of the way and for strengthening us for our next obstacles. Help us to continue to trust in You for strength, courage, and stamina as we travel along to our destination with You. We pray and say thanks for being our Waymaker, in Jesus' name, Amen.

REFLECTION

How would you use your story to encourage someone else?

DAY THIRTY THREE
A VERY PRESENT HELP

"God is our refuge and strength, a very present help in trouble."

Psalm 46:1 (KJV)

Solitary confinement for a two-month period allowed us to be more appreciative of freedom. The activities were planned, the route was mapped, the materials were prepared and the minds were set. My family and I got into the car to spend some well needed outside time. We had been in malice with the sun and have been hiding from outdoor social activities. This morning would be a change as the activities were exciting ones and everyone was interested to be a part.

I dropped my husband at the laundromat, and then my children and I drove three blocks away to a huge empty parking lot, which is vacant most of the time. The scheduled timetable was twenty-minute driving lessons for my son and twenty-minute riding lessons for my daughter. After that, I would call to confirm picking up my husband from the laundromat, and then we all would go food shopping.

At the end of the driving lesson, my son parked the car, took out the keys, and gave them to me. He sat in the car until the riding lesson was over. It was time for us to go, so I got in the driver's seat and tried to turn the ignition on. To my surprise, the key would not turn left or right. I tried again and again but got the same results.

I tried calling my husband's phone, but it went straight to voice mail. I questioned my son about his actions during the waiting period, and he assured me that he was just sitting in the car. I tried calling my husband's phone again about seven more times and got the same result – voicemail. I informed the children that we were going to pray and offered up a simple prayer. I tried the key again in the ignition again, but nothing changed. I sat there quietly for approximately ten minutes, waiting for God to answer as He always does. Shortly after, I looked at the entrance of the parking lot and saw my husband walking towards the car with the laundry basket in his hand. 'Thank you, Jesus!' I exclaimed. I smiled at the promise that I claimed and received in Psalm 46:1 (KJV), *"God is our refuge and strength, a very present help in trouble."*

We are reminded in this verse that God will help us in our time of need. He is our Tower of Strength and our Fortress whom we can run to for help, protection, and safety. My husband explained that his phone had died, and instead of waiting and not being able to hear from me, he decided to walk to where we were. After explaining to him what had happened with the car, he pushed the car once backward and then forward. He told me to turn the keys in the ignition, which I obeyed. To my amazement, the engine started. What a mighty God we serve! God knew that if I was able to drive to the laundromat, I would drive a different route. This would cause confusion in reuniting us, so He allowed me to stand still until my husband reached where we were.

Are you being forced to stand still in a situation that you are facing at this moment? Are you claiming God's promises while you wait? God is able to help us when we cry out to Him. He hears every time we call on Him and is excited to help His people. We do not need to stand in line and wait for our turn. We know that God is never tired of hearing our voice asking Him for help when we are in trouble. We know there is power in prayer, and as we continue to stand on God's promises, be encouraged that He will be present when we are in need of help.

TODAY'S PRAYER

Dear Lord, we thank You Mighty God for being no one else but God. We thank You for Your promises and never failing when we call on Your name for help. Lord, we thank You for being our help in the time of need. Help us to trust You continuously as we claim these promises. Help us to stay in Your presence at all times. Cover us with Your arms of love and mercy. We thank You for being with us always we pray in Jesus' name, Amen.

REFLECTION

What troubled time are you facing now that you need God's strength and help?

_____

_____

_____

_____

_____

_____

_____

_____

_____

_____

_____

DAY THIRTY FOUR
DECORATED CANVAS

"For we are God's masterpiece. He has created us anew in Christ Jesus, so we can do the good things he planned for us long ago."

Ephesians 2:10 (NLT)

I reflected on the blank canvas that once represented my life. It was fairly adequately sized but pure white, not a wrinkle or a spot. As time passed, it started to become real when I noticed some straight lines drawn on, which represented my extended family; then, I looked again and noticed some curly lines that represented my immediate family. Looking among those lines, I noticed that there were also dotted lines that represented my friends and some wavy lines that represented my church family. I was excited about these until I saw polka dots of many colors representing my successes, challenges, dreams, aspirations, and trials. Around each dot was an outer circle of the same color throughout all the dots. I wonder why? I thought to myself.

I continued looking, and then I noticed different shades of colors that represented the different seasons of my life. I also could identify the different abstracts and figured these were the many phases and stages of my life. There were some pictures I still could not recognize because these were the paths that I still had to take. The blessings were etched in my favorite color, red, which represents the blood that was shed for me on Calvary's cross. Every time I see that color, I remember that I am the apple of God's eye. Zechariah 2:8 (KJV)

I looked in the middle of the canvas, and there was a special shading aspect that represented my personality and character traits. This highlights my emotions, my integrity, my values, my character, and my morals. What a sight to behold, what a beauty. One that has never been seen before. *"For we are God's masterpiece. He has created us anew in Christ Jesus, so we can do the good things he planned for us long ago."* Ephesians 2:10 (NLT). The most important part that was noticed was the hand on the paintbrush.

No, you guessed it wrong. It was not my hand; it was not Ty's hand. BUT it was the hand of the Master. *"I praise you because I am fearfully and wonderfully made; your works are wonderful, I know that full well."* Psalm 139:14 (NIV). He is my Artist, and that outer circle around those polka dots that I couldn't recognize immediately was when He was carrying me through my journey. God highlights aspects of the ever-evolving canvas of our lives that are changing and growing us for the better: practices like praying through the challenges of finding the glimmers of beauty in what appears broken. I pray, and I am confident that He will never stop painting until my portrait is perfect in His sight and all that He planned for me will be evident on the canvas. May we continue to allow Him the opportunity to take control of the brush, paint, and canvas, trusting that His portrait of life's journeys and struggles is building the foundation for something truly magnificent.

TODAY'S PRAYER

Dear Lord, please cleanse us from our iniquities. Take our sins and cast them into the deepest parts of the sea and remember them no more. Thank You for being my Artist and for painting my masterpiece. Please continue working on me until my portrait is complete in Your eyes. Help me to be still so Your work will be done through me, for Your glory. I pray this in Jesus' name, Amen.

REFLECTION

If you were to visualize your portrait, what would it be like?

_____

_____

_____

_____

_____

_____

_____

_____

_____

_____

_____

_____

DAY THIRTY FIVE
MY KNIGHT IN SHINING ARMOR

"And he said, Hearken ye, all Judah, and ye inhabitants of Jerusalem, and thou king Jehoshaphat, Thus saith the Lord unto you, Be not afraid nor dismayed by reason of this great multitude; for the battle is not yours, but God's."

2 Corinthians 20:15 (KJV)

I watched carefully as little footsteps sprinted on the living room floors, with arms open wide, swaying from side to side. I prayed that no obstacle would cause an accident, especially the speed she was going. I was distracted by the sound of the words, 'I am your shining warmer,' which was repeatedly used to a tune I could not recognize. I continued to listen, trying to figure out the song or the phrase being dramatized by my three-year-old toddler. Finally, it dawned on me that she was not singing, 'You're my shining warmer,' but instead singing the words of a self-made song, 'You're my shining armor.'

That same weekend, all my mother's daughters had an encounter with a doctor due to different types of illnesses. I spoke with my older and younger sisters and tried as best as possible to encourage them while encouraging myself. We prayed together and felt motivated at the end of our conversation. Thank God, after a couple days, we were all feeling a little better. That's an improvement. That's the awesome power of prayer. Our Father is concerned about every detail of our lives, and when we speak to Him, He grants us the desires of our hearts. We have different battles placed before us, but we are reminded in Exodus 14:14 (KJV), *"The Lord will fight our battles for us."* This is comforting news.

Jesus is our 'Knight in shining armor,' and He will protect us, provide for us, heal us, and comfort us. He is our Creator, our Friend, our Great Physician, our Comforter, our Peace speaker, our Provider, and He is our everything. He is touched by the feelings of our infirmities, and He will always work things out according to what is best for us.

What battles are you trying to fight? What is your reason for needing a 'Knight in shining armor?' I encourage you to turn it over to Jesus. Accept and claim the promise given to us in 2 Corinthians 20:15 (KJV), *"Be not afraid nor dismayed by reason of this great multitude, for the battle is not yours but God's."* Give your battles to Him, stand still, and watch Him move in your life. There are times when we give our battles to Him and then take them back. He has never lost a battle. This time, give them totally to Him, and when you can't see His hand, just trust His heart. Let us allow Him to be our 'Knight in Shining Armor.'

TODAY'S PRAYER

Dear Lord, we thank You for being our everything. We ask that You help us to give our battles totally to You so You can fight them for us, and we can be confident that You're always victorious. Grant us peace. We pray with thanksgiving. In Jesus' name. Amen.

REFLECTION

What battles have you given to God and taken back? What will encourage you to give it totally to Him?

_____

_____

_____

_____

_____

_____

_____

_____

_____

_____

_____

_____

_____

DAY THIRTY SIX
LISTEN AND OBEY

"I listen carefully to what God the LORD is saying, for he speaks peace to his faithful people. But let them not return to their foolish ways."

Psalm 85:8 (NLT)

Buzzzz-zzz-zzzzzzzzz......I quickly grabbed the phone, startled by the vibration as it danced across the top of the night table. I was taking my well-needed daytime nap and had forgotten to turn my phone volume on silent. I recognized the number of my mentor and quickly answered the call. I was waiting to have a revision session with him to complete an assignment. To my disappointment, he wasn't calling to revise. As I listened to the words that came from his mouth and the tone in his voice, my disappointment changed to empathy immediately as he mentioned that his wife was in the hospital due to a stroke. I encouraged him and prayed with him and for his wife.

A couple days later, I was impressed to send a bouquet for her as I believed that would cheer her up. I discussed it with my husband, and he agreed. I researched florists near the hospital, and my eyes connected to the fifth item on the list. I called the hospital to confirm that they were accepting deliveries at this time, as well as to confirm her room number. I asked the representative at the hospital if they had deliveries from Florist A. She explained that they normally have floral deliveries, but it is unknown to her which companies do the deliveries. I was praying and hoping that the bouquet could be delivered the same day.

I started my investigation by calling Florist A, whose price range was within my budget, and the bouquets, even though pictures do not sometimes reflect a true picture of the actual thing - they were beautiful. I gave the representative my request, and without hesitation, he told me that the delivery would not be made until the next day. With disappointment, I continued my search. Florists B, C, and D were way out of my price range, and the floral arrangements were not as beautiful. I called them anyway. They all informed me that they were not able to do same-day deliveries but promised they could deliver very early the next morning. I had to make a decision. Since they all will do next-day delivery, I might as well go back to my first choice, Florist A. I placed my order, still a bit disappointed but praying that some change would be in place.

Approximately five minutes after the order, I got from Florist A to inform me that they would be able to deliver my order the same day. I was very happy to see how God knew what I wanted, and He was able to work it out in my favor. I was amazed at how, in obedience to the voice of the Holy Spirit, my desires were granted. David reminds us in Psalm 37:4 (KJV) that *"God will grant us the desires of our hearts."* Trusting God with the desires of our hearts requires faith in His provision. It's acknowledging that He is our ultimate source of wisdom, guidance, and resources. He will open doors no man can shut and shut doors no man can open. He will provide opportunities and connect us to the right people to help us realize our desires. As we cultivate a heart that finds joy, satisfaction, and contentment in God, He will transform our desires to reflect His purposes. While the fulfillment of our desires may not always align with our expectations, we can trust in the faithfulness of God. By embracing the promise in Psalm (37:4), our lives become characterized by the fulfillment of desires that bring glory to Him. Are you waiting in anticipation for God to work something out in your favor? Trust Him, ask Him, claim the promises that He has given us, and watch Him work it all out.

TODAY'S PRAYER

Dear God, thank You for knowing the desires of our hearts and granting them to us. Thank You for speaking to us and directing us. Please grant us the Spirit of discernment so we will be able to identify Your voice, and help us to be obedient to Your words. You are an awesome God, and we praise You in Jesus' name. Amen.

REFLECTION

Do you always obey the still, small voice? Explain a situation where you were obedient to God's voice, and things worked out in your favor?

_____

_____

_____

_____

_____

_____

_____

_____

_____

_____

_____

_____

DAY THIRTY SEVEN
I AM ALONE BUT NOT LONELY

"The LORD your God is with you, the Mighty Warrior who saves. He will take great delight in you; in his love he will no longer rebuke you, but will rejoice over you with singing."

Zephaniah 3:17 (NIV)

Have you ever felt like you are alone? Not lonely but that you are alone. I am in the house with my family, but I am Alone. When the pain rocks my body from side to side, and my family and friends look on with empathy and sympathy, I am Alone. When I am going through my crucibles, and they are there to love and support me, I am Alone. When I am traveling on rugged terrain, and I don't know what to expect next, I am Alone. When I pray, and they pray, for and with me, I am Alone. When my body turns inside out, and they secretly cry for me, I am Alone.

When I no longer eat the foods they eat because my diet is totally different, I am Alone. When my clothes don't fit anymore, I am Alone. When I cry myself to sleep at night, I am Alone.

When my features change, and I don't look like the same person that I am used to seeing in the mirror, I am Alone. I AM ALONE, not because my family and friends don't pray for and visit me, empathize, sympathize, love, and support me. They can only imagine. They cannot fully understand unless they experience the same thing. Even in that case, they might react to the situation differently.

I AM ALONE BUT NEVER LONELY. I am alone, but thank God that Jesus walked this lonesome valley before me. No one else could walk it for Him. He gives me hope, joy, and assurance when He promised me in Isaiah 43:2 (NIV), *"When you pass through the waters, I will be with you, and when you pass through the rivers, they will not sweep over you. When you walk through the fire, you will not be burned, the flames will not set you ablaze."*

Do you feel like you are travelling alone on this journey? Are you experiencing a situation that no one else understands? Whatever situation we feel, God comes to us. He meets us in our alone state. He is with us through pain and through our tears, through our cries and through sighs. Whatever our circumstances are, God has a purpose for our lives. He simply wants us to trust him even when we feel alone. In our aloneness, we are encouraged to call out to God, and He will hear our cries and answer our call. God is not limited to our alone times, and He will be with us no matter what our circumstances are. He simply wants us to trust Him as He works out His will for our lives. Matthew 28:20 (KJV) tells us, *"...I am with you always even to the end of the world." Jesus is with us always, and He will never leave us nor forsake us.*

TODAY'S PRAYER

Dear Jesus, purge us with hyssop and make us clean. Thank You for helping us to know that with You, we are never alone and that You are always with us. Continue to help us as we trust in Your presence and Your will for us, in Jesus' name. Amen.

REFLECTION

How do you reach out to God when you feel alone?

DAY THIRTY EIGHT
JUST FOR YOU

"But they that wait upon the LORD shall renew their strength; they shall mount up with wings as eagles; they shall run, and not be weary; and they shall walk, and not faint.

Isaiah 40:31 (KJV)

God's desire was for us to live a perfect life where happiness was never limited. However, the fall of man came, and sin came on the earth, which caused a constant battle for those who chose to follow Jesus. You are fearfully and wonderfully made; you are called out from among everyone else, and so God asked the enemy if he had considered His servant **(INSERT YOUR NAME HERE)**. He knew your character and your growth in him. He knew that even though you will bend through all the hurt and the pain, through all the hate and the lies, through all the disappointments and the tears, you will not break. When you were created, He mixed an extra layer of strength in you that you or no one else knows about, and so no matter what storm comes your way, no matter what wind blows, no matter what rain falls down on you that you might be covered for a short while but you will never completely disappear because of that strength that He himself placed in you.

The enemy will attack, the enemy is attacking, and the enemy will continue to attack but continue to draw strength from His promises. When the enemy comes at you, determine in your heart that you will speak God's promises to your inner me. Promises such as:

Exodus 14:14 (KJV) *"The LORD shall fight for you, and ye shall hold your peace."*

2 Chronicles 20:15 (ESV) *"Thus says the LORD to you, 'Do not be afraid and do not be dismayed at this great horde, for the battle is not yours but God's."*

2 Corinthians 12:9 (NKJV), *and He said to me, "My grace is sufficient for*

you, for My strength is made perfect in weakness."

Isaiah 43:2 (KJV), *"When thou passest through the waters, I will be with thee; and through the rivers, they shall not overflow thee: when thou walkest through the fire, thou shalt not be burned; neither shall the flame kindle upon thee."*

The Lord will never leave us nor forsake us, Isaiah 40:31 (KJV), *"But they that wait upon the LORD shall renew their strength; they shall mount up with wings as eagles; they shall run, and not be weary; and they shall walk, and not faint. I could go on and on."*

Continue to draw strength from those who have gone on before us, as well as those around us who are claiming and receiving these promises every day. Whatever you are going through right now is just for a season. It is only for a period. Each season that you go through is important as it prepares you for the next one. It also strengthens your faith to know that you will come through, just as how you were able to pull through the previous season. In the end, you will begin a new season. This gives you hope. You will reap the harvest that God has promised you. God is doing a new thing in you. He will even make rivers run in the desert.

Know that you are His favorite, the apple of His eyes, to the extent that when He was on the cross, you were on His mind. He has carried you before, He is carrying you now, and He will continue to carry you. Just trust His plans, as they will all work out for your good. God comes that you may have life and that you may have it more abundantly. That is life eternal. Hold on, as God will make a way out of no way.

TODAY'S PRAYER

Dear God, thank You for never leaving us alone and for staying true to Your promises. Thank You for always making a way out of no way and changing the impossible into I'm possible. Help us to trust You always as we continue to grow in Your strength. Keep our eyes fixed on You as we walk through all seasons of life with the comfort that You are taking us through. We lift You up as our Lord and Savior and cling to You, in Jesus' name, Amen.

REFLECTION

What season are you going through presently, and what new thing are you expecting God to do for you?

_____
_____
_____
_____
_____
_____
_____
_____
_____
_____
_____
_____

DAY THIRTY NINE
'PATIENCE AND TRUST' - LESSONS LEARNED

"But if we look forward to something we don't yet have, we must wait patiently and confidently."

Romans 8:25 (NLT)

'What will the next move be?' I pondered the question asked by my girlfriend very deeply but was provided with no answer. I quickly sent my resume to the provided email address as soon as I saw that they had a vacancy. I thought that this was something that I was very comfortable doing. It seemed like a difficult job, but I liked challenges and knew I would be an asset. I checked my email early the next morning to see if I had received a response, but there was nothing there yet. The next day, I opened up with anticipation and was excited to see that I was being considered for the job. I was required to complete an eight-hour course. I completed my course, passed my exam with a full score, and submitted my certification. I waited for another three months with no correspondence from the company. At one point, I was even thinking of not accepting if I received a call. It has been a year and a half after I was terminated from my job due to illness. My family has been tremendously blessed with a wonderful support group that also helped us financially. After a while, that subsided, which we are grateful for, and we realized that God had someone else who needed assistance, and the focus was now diverted to a different direction. With this break in the finance chain, I was forced to apply for assistance through the unemployment system. I was never one to use those services as my thoughts were that I was independent and healthy, and I believe those services were provided for people who really needed assistance. I am very independent but fell into a season of dependence, and after much counsel and advice, I decided to apply. I was approved and reaped the benefits for a while. The question came at the final week of my assistance when my girlfriend asked the question out of curiosity and concern. 'You don't get support from your group anymore, and your assistance is ending. What is the next plan that God has for you?' I replied with confidence that I really don't know, but I am sure He has a plan, let's wait and see.'

Our concern and curiosity turned into reality when I received a call a couple days after that conversation to inform me that I was offered a vacancy for the position that I had applied for five months ago. I thought about the entire process, the questions that were asked a couple days prior and the fact that I would be able to work from home.

Are you in your waiting period? What are the emotions that you are experiencing during this period? Do you feel like God is holding out on you? We all are faced with situations sometimes where our patience is tried. Being patient is very important in trusting God. We can always turn to God for help as we wait on His timing and trust His plans for our lives. Psalm 27:14 (KJV) reminds us that we should *"Wait on the Lord: be of good courage, and he shall strengthen thine heart: wait, I say on the Lord."* Another promise we can claim comes to us from Isaiah 40: 31 (KJV), *"but they that wait upon the Lord, shall renew their strength; they shall mount up with wings as eagles; they shall run and not be weary; and they shall walk and not faint."* God will always come true for us at the right time, which is always the best time. He knows the desires of our heart, will grant them unto us, and will complete what He started. Let us trust Him with our whole heart as He continues to teach us lessons of patience and trust through our experiences.

TODAY'S PRAYER

Dear Lord, we come to You thanking You for the lessons You teach us and will continue to teach us. We pray for patience as we continue to trust You with our lives. Help us learn the lessons that You seek to teach us and help us execute the content learned. Continue to work on and in us until we are who You want us to be. Help us to be obedient to Your words as we continue to claim Your promises over our lives; we pray and say thank You, in Jesus' name, Amen.

REFLECTION

What waiting period are you in at this moment, and how can you encourage yourself not to get discouraged?

_____

_____

_____

_____

_____

_____

_____

_____

_____

_____

_____

_____

DAY FORTY
GOD HAS THE FINAL WORD

"Many plans are in a person's heart, But the advice of the Lord will stand."
Proverbs 19:21 (NASB)

I have been keeping up with my appointments and have been getting my treatments on time. Injections can be referred to as my foe, but due to my illness, I am trying to promote them to friend status. We have to cross paths ever so often due to my infusions, but I still smirk at even the very sight of the needle. I put on a brave face as I am injected yet another time. The post-feelings appeared as usual, but I tried very hard to ignore them. It was not very long after an episode that I received a call from my doctor. With a regular greeting, she asked how I was feeling. I smiled and replied that I was doing well. I returned the question to her, hoping for the same answer, but was disappointed when she informed me that she was concerned for me. My features changed at that comment, and my ears opened wider as I anticipated the next information that she had to share with me. *'Your body has rejected the medication that you are presently on, even though you are improving, and we have to change it,'* she continued. I have been on this particular medication for the past ten months, and it has been controlling my illness very well. I continued listening with mixed emotions. I have suffered tremendously with excruciating pain along with other unpleasant attachments to this illness and had no desire to repeat that part of my history. She explained briefly the next treatments of consideration and implored me to research and think about them so we could make a decision. She also gave directions as to different actions that will be taken prior to the new treatment that will be administered to me.

I did what I knew would help me feel better after this conversation. I prayed and took a long, hot shower. I knew I had no control, so I had to give it to Him who controls my life. I reminded myself that I was the apple of God's eye, and he told me to reason with Him. Isaiah 1:18 (NASB) tells me clearly, *"Come now let us reason together,' Says the Lord, though your sins be as scarlet, they shall be white as snow, though they be red like crimson, they shall be as wool."*

Still keeping my prior treatment date, I continued with the course of action and completed all that I had to do before my next treatment. My doctor and I communicated each time I completed an assignment, but there was never any confirmation of what the new treatment would be.

I arrived at my scheduled location for treatment and checked in. The nurse escorted me to my assigned area and did the necessary questioning. After I settled in, she wanted to confirm the treatment that I was receiving. When she checked the information that she had and called to confirm the change with the doctor, no change was documented. Sad to say that if I did a repeat of the old treatment, I would go into regression. I left the office without being treated, and the good thing is that I am not experiencing any symptoms due to my illness. I am comforted by the fact that my God knows exactly what he has ordained for my life, and He will allow that plan to work. Do you feel disappointed because something did not work according to your plan? Are you in a moment of wondering why? Have you been stuck between two decisions and don't know which is the right choice? There may be times when you feel like there is no help, no answer, or no hope, but God makes the best decisions for our lives. He comes through at the right time, and He has the final say. God's timing is perfect; it strengthens and grows our faith. He is never late, and our timing is not God's timing. During the waiting time, we experience growth in patience, trust, and faith. At the moment when God comes through for us, we have to give Him all the glory. Psalm 31:15 (NIV) says, *"My times are in your hands..."* There are times when we experience a situation, and we put periods in our lives. When we place everything in God's hands, we realize that these are the moments when He puts a comma, as He wants to complete the work that He has started. Let us praise Him through our pain and our waiting. Be encouraged that at the right time, God will provide your needs, He will heal you from all sickness, He will be your lawyer, He will deliver you, and He will rescue you. At the right time, God will show up, and in His time, He will complete what He started in your life.

TODAY'S PRAYER

Dear Jesus, thank You for teaching us how to wait on Your timing. Please grant us patience, faith, and trust while we await Your timing and will for our lives. Help us to praise You through our pain as You continue to turn our pressure into praise and our worry into worship. Complete what You started in us, as we trust in Your timing. We say thanks for hearing, helping, and delivering us in Jesus' name, Amen.

REFLECTION

In what ways do you show praise through your pain, and what 'why' moment are you experiencing?

_____

_____

_____

_____

_____

_____

_____

_____

_____

_____

_____

_____

ABOUT THE AUTHOR

Sandrean is a wife, mother, speaker, and dedicated Christian. A teacher by profession who has spent over ten years in the classroom. She has a passion for imparting knowledge and helping and encouraging others. She is actively engaged as a volunteer at a local prison ministry and in other community service activities. Prayer is the most important part of her life, and she sincerely believes that prayer changes things for her and everyone else. She gets excited whenever she gets the privilege to share the goodness of God with others. Her desire is to introduce others to Christ and to continue to grow into the person God intends for her to be as she continues to walk in and grow in His divine calling for her life. She has been impressed to share her personal experiences, even though there have been many ups and downs. It is through these experiences that she seeks to motivate others, too – *"Trust in the Lord with all thine heart; and lean not unto thine own understanding. In all thy ways, acknowledge Him and He shall direct thy path."* Proverbs 3:5-6 (KJV)

CHECK OUT THIS BOOK BY THE AUTHOR

Our children hear from various influences who they should be. Television, film, internet, social media, society and even educators advise them how to view themselves. Affirmations are very important on a daily basis as this is one method that will help to build self-confidence. Using simple affirmations to our children can help them to think positively about themselves from an early age and this will help them to become grounded adults. Repeating the words in this book to our children will have a lifetime positive effect on building their character. We are all created differently. No two persons are alike. 'Be You' is targeted to children who are zero to twelve years old and aim to help to teach parents to remind children that even though each person is different and is at a different level in life to just be whom they are.

ISBN: 978-1-964972-03-9
BE YOU is available everywhere books are sold.

Milton Keynes UK
Ingram Content Group UK Ltd.
UKHW051059260824
447446UK00013B/982